Be Cool. 54

Giuseppe Zanini

The book of
WHEN

TREASURE PRESS

Contributors:

Andrea Bonanni   Pinuccia Bracco
Glauco Pretto

Text adapted by
Christine Casley

First published in Great Britain in 1986 by
The Hamlyn Publishing Group Limited

This edition published in 1989 by
Treasure Press
Michelin House, 81 Fulham Road
London SW3 6RB

ISBN 1 85051 375 9

Printed in Czechoslovakia
52114/3

INTRODUCTION

These books are intended to answer the many questions of a historical nature which crop up in the minds of children for thousands of different reasons. They delve back into the past, searching for fragments of information which are often left out of the history books. Such details can arouse more curiosity and interest than great events which, although they may have changed the world, can be dry and off-putting when they have to be studied compulsorily.

The layout of the text, the simple vocabulary, short chapters and the choice of strange or outstanding facts make the books both easy and pleasant to read. Their colourful illustrations are another way of stimulating interest and they will be eagerly consulted, read or simply glanced through by young and old alike. Everyone will find some new or unusual item of information which will make him want to read on and maybe find out more about it. One of the main aims will have been achieved if the variety and brevity of the topics makes the reader rediscover history in a less solemn but certainly more lively, pleasant and even amusing form. The history will therefore not only be of men and wars but also of the world, life, things great and things small, minor inventions and major ones, animals, plants and rocks.

In planning these books, the intention was obviously not to present a complete and organic whole, less still to compile a systematic encyclopedia. The purpose was and is to answer some queries while encouraging others. If an occasional glance through the pages makes the young reader feel how scanty his knowledge is and how much he would like to broaden it, the books will have fulfilled their task. This is, in short, partly to satisfy some of the immediate desire to learn, but mostly to open up wider horizons and lead to broader, more intensive examination of specific subjects. Such study will meet the needs of the more enquiring and receptive young minds who want to deepen their own knowledge of subjects only dealt with here in brief.

CONTENTS

WHEN THE WORLD BEGAN

Millions of stars are to be seen scattered in the sky on clear nights. There are many more, however, which are invisible to the naked eye and can only be detected with powerful telescopes. The millions and millions of bright dots everywhere in space are really vast numbers of stars called galaxies.

Our world also belongs to a galaxy. The Sun, around which the Earth rotates, is a small star travelling at high speed on the edge of the spiral-shaped galaxy called by the ancients the Milky Way. The other stars which travel

About 4,500 million years ago, in a spinning cloud of gas and cosmic dust, some of the nuclei condensed. As they rotated they gradually gathered up the surrounding matter, growing larger and larger and more and more solid.

with us in the universe and which therefore belong to the same galaxy, form a broad band in the sky, so thickly scattered with lights that it makes a milky glow in the dark. It is from this that it takes its name, the Milky Way.

When and how were all these stars formed? It is difficult to give a precise answer but it seems that they all originate from the condensation of white-hot gases, the first and oldest 'matter' in the universe. The solar system, that is the Sun and the planets in orbit round it, was also created from a spinning cloud of gas. This itself was a tiny part of the enormous cloud of white-hot gases from which all the stars in the Milky Way originated.

According to recent discoveries, our Milky Way began to form some 10,000 million years ago. As time passed the gases of which it consisted condensed into a great many nuclei, or cores, each of which became a star.

The Sun, which is the nearest star to us, began to form 4,500 million years ago. From the outer portions of the gaseous cloud which formed the Sun the planets were born, including the Earth.

When the Earth was born

If we look back through the history of the Earth, we come to a time, hundreds of millions of years ago, when there was no sign of life on our planet. If we go back still further in time, we reach a mysterious period when the Earth emerged like a ball of fire from a mass of white-hot gases and moved away into space, turning continuously round the shining Sun. Perhaps we will never know exactly when and how our planet was born but it most probably did begin like this.

About 4,500 million years ago, in a spinning cloud of gas and dust, some of the nuclei condensed. As they rotated they gradually gathered up the surrounding matter, growing larger and larger and more and more solid. The central nucleus became the Sun while the others gave rise to the various planets of the solar system.

Under the influence of the force of the Earth's gravity and the enormous atmospheric pressure, the cosmic dust (high speed radioactive particles) falling from space to form the Earth heated up until it became white-hot. The inner core of our planet is still white-hot today.

The Earth emerged like a ball of fire from a mass of white-hot gases

If we could cut the Earth in two we would see that it is formed of a rocky outer crust, some 40 kilometres thick, of a second inner mantle of iron and magnesium silicates 2,900 kilometres deep and of a central core of white-hot, molten iron 6,700 kilometres across. This core probably produces the Earth's magnetic field.

The vertical and horizontal projection of our galaxy. The arrows show the position of the solar system.

When the Earth solidified

One of the most difficult tasks of geology (the science or study of the Earth), has been to establish the age of the Earth. Until about fifty years ago the scientists had little information to help them with this problem. By careful observation they could discover whether one rock was older than another, but the further back they went in time, the more hazy and uncertain their knowledge became.

It was only with the discovery of radioactivity that geology made a great step forward in this field.

By studying certain radioactive substances, it was discovered that, in the course of time, they lose

their radioactivity at a steady, invariable rate. The element uranium, for example, loses its radioactive properties over a very long period of time and changes into lead. We know that one gramme of uranium takes a thousand years to produce 1/7,000,000 of a gramme of lead. With this knowledge it is possible to calculate the age of a rock containing uranium by comparing the amount of lead produced in it with the amount of uranium still present.

Tests made on radioactive rocks all over the world have shown that the oldest were formed about 3,800 million years ago. However, from the ages of meteorites, the Earth is thought to have formed about 4,500 million years ago.

When the first rocks were formed

In the violent beginnings of our planet the surface of the Earth looked a terrifying place. White-hot magma, formed of molten rock from the Earth's interior, boiled on the surface with constant explosions. At the same time showers of meteorites and cosmic dust, attracted by the pull of the Earth's gravity, made the sphere grow bigger and bigger as it rotated in space.

Huge spirals of gas and water vapour rose out of the magma to darken the sky and keep the light of the Sun from falling on to the Earth. The gloom of the night was continually shattered by flashes from the explosions and eruptions of the Earth's surface.

Millions of years passed before the first islands of rock, derived from cooled magma, appeared on the sea of lava. As it solidified, the white-hot magma, which formed the Earth in the beginning, gave rise to a basic rock type known as igneous (from the Latin *ignis*, meaning fire). There is little trace left of these rocks today, however, at least on the surface: corroded and wasted away by the forces present in the atmosphere, they have been transformed into gravel, fine sand and dust.

These substances, washed away into the large sea-basins by rivers and floods, have been deposited there in layers. The weight of the upper layers exerted tremendous pressure on those beneath, squeezing out the water and then cementing the fragments together again, forming new rocks. By the action of intense natural forces, they have then undergone other fundamental changes. The layers, or strata, have been folded, curved or broken. The distorted layerings of the rocks on our mountains give some idea of what happened to the Earth's crust.

When the first mountains were formed

As it gradually cooled, the magma solidified on the surface and the Earth became covered with a crust of primeval rocks, mainly consisting of granite and basalt. These rocks encased our globe like a rigid shell, while inside it continued to be burning hot.

When the Earth cooled still more it shrank, and the rocky layer which covered it had to contract, like an apple whose skin wrinkles as it withers.

The shell of primeval rocks wrinkled and folded under the strong lateral pressures caused by this shrinking. In some places it sank into the underlying magma; in others it rose up towards the sky.

That is how the first mountains were formed but there is no trace of them left today. Countless disturbances over the ages have completely destroyed them. The mountains we admire today are from later periods and in some cases are comparatively recent.

When water appeared on the Earth

The first folds in the crust of the Earth took place in complete darkness, when the world still felt very hot. The Earth had cooled sufficiently to harden the rocks but its temperature was still far higher than that of boiling water.

No water was to be found on the surface and all the water vapour coming from the burning cracks in the ground collected in enormous masses of clouds, tens of kilometres thick, which completely darkened the sky.

Even if any vapour was occasionally changed into rain by the strong condensation, the falling drops vaporized again as soon as they touched the burning hot surface of the Earth. So the sky of our planet was permanently clouded by masses of swirling vapour.

There came a time, however, when the rocks had cooled down sufficiently so that the water no longer boiled as it touched them. This is when the rain began to fall. For thousands and thousands of years the large masses of clouds had held back the water which had gushed out of the depths of the Earth. Now they poured it back on its mountains and plains.

It rained and it rained, without stopping, for centuries. It was the greatest flood of all time.

When the oceans were formed

When the crust of the Earth eventually cooled, there began the most tremendous erosion of its surface rocks.

Under the non-stop, pelting rain, the softer rocks broke up and were swept away. The first valleys were formed, along which the sheets of water rushed towards the largest hollows in the surface of the Earth. Here it collected as it fell from the sky or ran down off the mountains. The hollows filled up and became wider and wider water basins from which islands and erupting volcanoes appeared. And so the first seas and the primeval oceans were formed.

The greatest development of the oceans took place at the start of the Palaeozoic Era, which was the time of the great rains. Whole continents were submerged by the water, which spread over much of the Earth's surface.

The rule of the seas lasted for another hundred million years, through the Cambrian and into the Ordovician Period. A new series of major foldings of the Earth's crust then began, forcing up great mountain chains. The formation of the mountains of Scandinavia, Scotland and Ireland dates back to this period.

Diagrammatic section through the ocean floor, with the main features

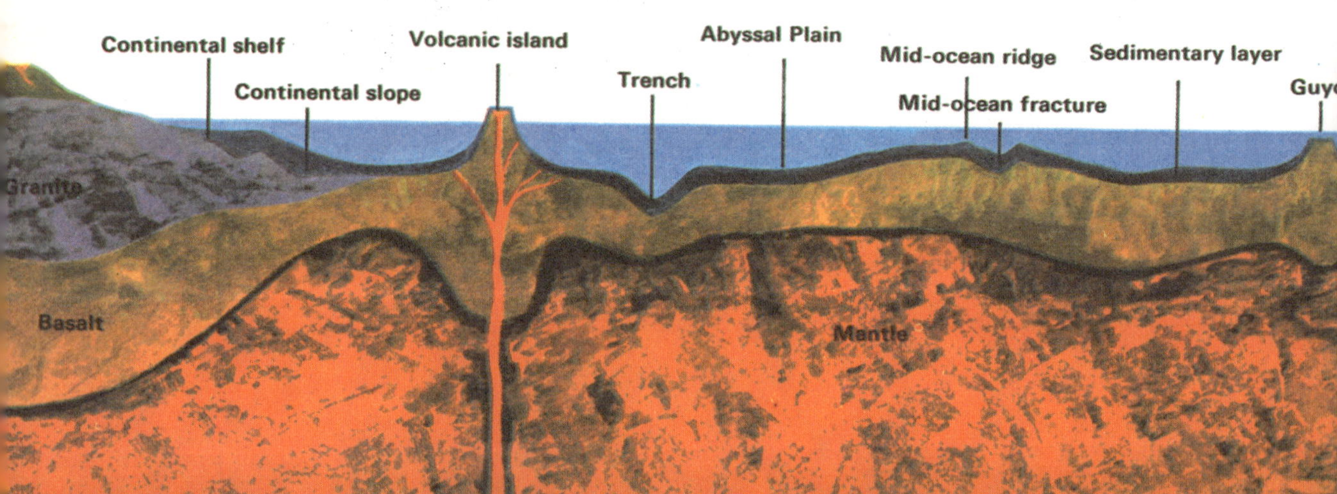

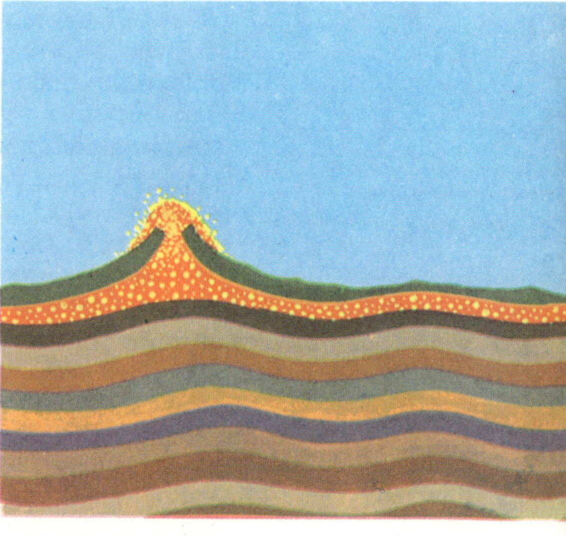

The vapour collected in the rock strata then broke through to the surface, giving rise to volcanoes

When the Earth was covered with sand and gravel

As soon as the great rains had finished the black clouds disappeared from the sky. Yet the fury of the water which had worn away the mountains did not subside or vanish in the vast basins of the oceans. Now, it was not only the driving rain and flowing rivers which eroded the land. When the wind blew the water covering the submerged continents grew rough. It rose up in great waves which battered and pounded the coast and the islands. Even the strongest rocks gave way under the blows and disintegrated into fine grains of sand, which were then carried far away.

For several million years the erosive action of the water wore away all the rocks which had been formed as the white-hot magma cooled. The thick strata which had formed the original crust of the Earth disappeared, destroyed by the fury of the waters. At the same time, however, new rocks were being formed. The sands produced by the erosion and piled high, layer upon layer, were compressed together and transformed into firm, compact rock by the action of the various forces in the atmosphere. The surface of the Earth could not be without its crust of rocks and the new ones, the first of sedimentary origin, replaced the old, together with others which had been formed by more recent cooling of the volcanic magma.

The oldest rocks known today, such as the Ayers Rock in Australia, are, in fact, sedimentary sandstones, formed of fine grains of sand which have been cemented together again into compact rock.

When lava covered vast areas of land

Volcanic activity was particularly intense in the beginnings of the Earth. The boiling magma underneath the Earth's crust had to find a way out to the surface. Vast areas of land were covered with thick layers of lava and it even invaded the floors of the seas. Sometimes there was so much lava that it formed big islands standing up above sea-level.

In the Devonian Period 405 to 340 million years ago, which followed the Silurian, the foldings of the Earth's crust continued and three large land masses emerged from the sea: the Siberian, the Equatorial and the North Atlantic.

A study of the rocks formed in this period suggests that Africa was linked to South America in one huge continent covered with folds.

The shiftings of the Earth's crust ended in the Carboniferous Period, which lasted from 340 to 260 million years ago, when the central areas of Europe, Asia and North America rose up.

The oldest rocks of this period show signs of tremendous earthquakes, of great upheavals which made whole continents sink into the oceans, of terrible floods and gigantic eruptions. The rock strata, in fact, reflect what powerful forces of nature were let loose on our young planet. Nevertheless until the Devonian Period when amphibians evolved and the first seed plants appeared, they are silent if we ask what forms of life they witnessed on land.

When life was born in the sea

Life first began in the sea. The earliest living beings were certainly minute creatures, very simple in structure, but they had one ability which neither water nor air nor rocks possessed: they were capable of reproducing. They could breed beings similar to themselves.

Were the first living beings animals? Or were they plants? They were really neither one thing nor the other because their way of life was completely different from that of the present inhabitants of the animal and plant kingdom. These first microscopic life-forms were simple little balls of jelly, known as flagellata. They gradually acquired the ability to use the energy of the Sun to feed themselves and grow.

They then developed into different groups, some becoming the first single-celled plants and others the first single-celled animals, called the protozoa. They joined up into colonies, forming gelatinous masses which later gave rise to many-celled animals and plants.

The algae were the first forms of plant-life with well-defined characteristics. The various types of algae inhabited all the seas and were the first link in the chain of life.

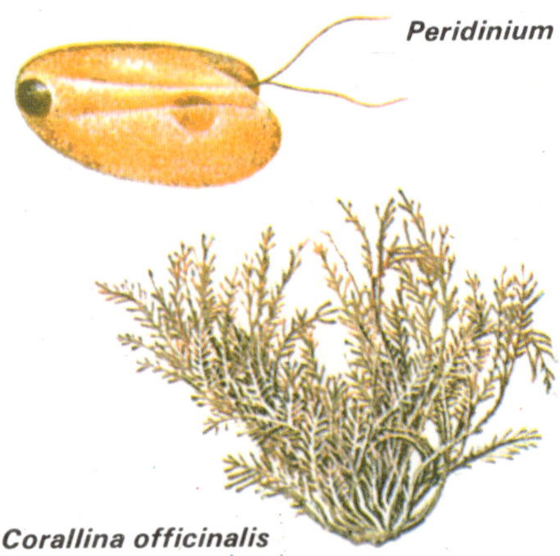

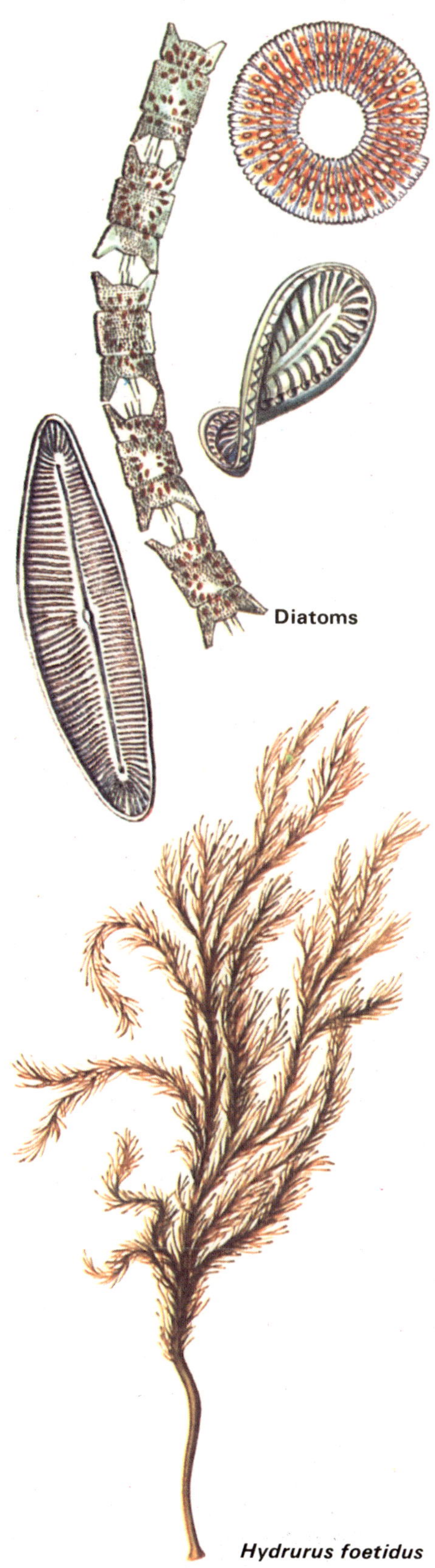

Diatoms

Hydrurus foetidus

When there was no life on land

For life in the sea the surrounding conditions were particularly favourable and it developed rapidly. The tiny single-celled beings grew into more complex animals and plants and, by the start of the Palaeozoic Era, animals like the nautiloids (enormous snails), and sponges, starfish, jellyfish and shellfish had already appeared in the waters. Seaweeds also flourished.

While the seas were bustling with intense activity, however, the land looked lifeless. Not a blade of grass grew on the worn, weather-beaten mountains or on the plains devastated by the swollen rivers. No insects flew in the gloomy primeval skies, still frequently heavy with rain.

Everywhere was silent and deserted: hundreds of thousands of years were to pass before dry land could begin to be inhabited, to be covered with a mantle of plants, to support the first little animals, to know life. The earliest living things to appear on land were mosses very similar to those we see today.

When coal was formed

The first living beings to succeed in leaving the sea and adapting themselves to life in the air were the algae, simple water-dwelling plants. From these more complex plants were then evolved.

Once they had adapted to their new surroundings, the plants developed quickly. They invaded the land and covered it with green. The period which saw the greatest growth of the forests was the Carboniferous, so called because it was then, 300 million years ago, that the large coal seams were formed.

The black pieces of coal still used today in industry and for heating many homes therefore have a history dating from that time. They were formed by the decomposition of the forests which then covered the surface of the Earth. As time passed, the enormous trunks, felled by age or storms, formed thick layers of wood which were then buried under layers of mud and sand. Instead of rotting, the wood changed completely, partly because it was no longer in contact with the air and partly because of the tremendous pressures and heat of the Earth.

All that remains of the ancient forests are the seams of pit-coal under the ground.

There are several types of coal, depending on their age and the conditions in which they were formed. The most important are bituminous coal and anthracite. Coal-gas and gas for domestic purposes were recovered from bituminous coal. Coke is a by-product. Anthracite gives great heat with little ash and is therefore mostly used for heating systems.

When oil was formed

Today coal has lost the lead it once enjoyed among the fuels. First place has been taken by oil, the precious substance which gushes out of the depths of the Earth, bringing wealth and prosperity to the countries where it is found.

In his search for oil, man has managed to make even the desert habitable, to build enormous platforms to float on the sea, to drill through rock strata down to depths of some 5,000 metres, and has spent enormous sums in doing so.

These are always handsomely repaid once an oil-field has been reached, however, for tons and tons of 'black gold' (as oil is called) stream out of the well. The oil is taken through pipelines to refineries or tankers.

Oil is generally younger than coal. Its formation dates back to a more recent period in the history of the Earth, to the Mesozoic Era, which lasted 225 million to 65 million years ago. This era saw the rise and fall of the great dinosaurs.

Even in the Mesozoic Era the folding and settling of the Earth's crust continued. Thick deposits of sea and lake sediment accumulated in different parts of the globe. The way in which these deposits are layered shows that the land and seas were successively rising and falling in this period.

The Cretaceous Period, from 130 million to 65 million years ago, takes its name from the French word *craie*, meaning chalk, which was actually formed in those distant times. This period is one of the longest in the history of the Earth. It lasted for over 65 million years, during which animal-life on land developed in profusion.

Some of the most important oil

and natural gas fields discovered in Canada and the United States are to be found in the rocks of the Cretaceous Period. Because of the unsettled conditions on Earth, enormous masses of organic substances, perhaps derived from decomposing animals, were imprisoned in the ground where they were gradually transformed until they became the mineral oils of today.

The rock strata of this period are very important, partly because they contain large deposits of copper, aluminium and other minerals but mostly because they also contain fossil traces of the first flowers, a sign that great progress was being made in the plant kingdom.

When the present continents were formed

At the very time when oil was beginning to form, an enormous shift took place in the Earth's crust, which slowly resulted in the formation of the present continents.

Numerous studies, even in recent years, confirm the theory that the great continental mass pushed out of the sea in the earlier periods and then split apart into several pieces which drifted about the Earth for hundreds of millions of years. Finally, between the middle of Cretaceous and early Tertiary Periods (100 million to 50 million years ago) these pieces split up again to form land masses recognizable in form to the continents of today. These sections are still drifting apart.

This interesting suggestion, first put forward by the German meteorologist, Alfred Wegener (1880–1930), is known as the theory of 'continental drift'.

Wegener, who was also a daring explorer and experienced geologist, published his ideas in a book printed in 1912. It naturally created a great stir in scientific circles, which soon split into two

groups, one of his supporters and one of his opponents. They were both eager to prove or disprove his theory.

In a few words, Wegener's idea was as follows: in dim, distant times the continental masses were joined together in a single block (or shield), which Wegener called Pangaea. The rest of the Earth was covered by a primeval mass of water, the Pantalaxia.

During the Eocene Period, about 50 million years ago, a slow but steady movement then began. The Pangaea cracked and, pulled apart by the rotating movement of the Earth, the bits began to drift away from each other as if they were floating on a heavier, more elastic base.

According to Wegener, it was because of this shifting that the folds occurred in the Earth's crust which lifted up the loftiest mountain chains still existing in the world today.

When America broke away from Africa

A careful look at the maps in an atlas will help support Wegener's theory. A map of the Atlantic Ocean, for example, shows a striking similarity in the shape of the two coastlines, one on the Eurafrican side and the other on the American. It almost seems as if the pieces would fit together.

If we believe that the land was once adrift in a single piece on the surface of the Earth, then Eurafrica and America must have slowly floated away from each other.

Apart from the geographical proof, which could be attributed to a vivid imagination, there is surprising geological evidence based on careful study of the rocks. The structure of the minerals both on the Atlantic coast and on the other coasts concerned in the drift theory, shows that not only do they have the same properties but there are even signs of events which occurred before the fracture (folds and ridges).

The animal-life also has strangely similar features: certain animals, like the earth-worms, the snails and some shallow-water fish, lived along both the Eurafrican and the

Extent of the Arctic ice-cap today (above) and in the Great Ice Age (below)

American coasts. The same applies to certain plants.

There is even indisputable geodetic evidence (geodesy is the science of measuring the shape and size of the Earth) to show that the drift is still continuing today. As late as the last century it was suggested that Greenland was moving. It is now known that it is drifting away from Europe at about 2 centimetres a year. The other 'suspect' lands are also continuing to be measured. It is believed that a crack in Africa is working its way along the line of the river Nile and the Great Lakes. Perhaps in hundreds of thousands of years Africa will have broken off, too.

How the Earth may have looked in a cold, glacial period and a warmer, interglacial period of the Pleistocene Era

When the ice invaded the land

About 38 million years ago, when the first large mammals were living on Earth, the climate underwent a great change. In the Oligocene Period, 38 to 27 million years ago, it was still warm and temperate but in the Miocene which followed it grew colder, affecting the spread of the plants. Many tropical or subtropical types of plant disappeared and even the woods shrank, to be replaced by immense grassy plains.

The effects of this change on animal evolution were far-reaching. Many mammals who had been used to feeding on the shoots of trees and bushes had to adapt to feeding on grass. This led to their gradual transformation, which was particularly noticeable in the

shape of their teeth and the structure of their feet and necks.

In the Miocene Period, the mountain chains which had begun to emerge in the earlier periods continued to be lifted up. New land surfaced above the sea, with the result that the oceans shrank. These movements were completed in the Pliocene Period (the last in the Cenozoic Era), which lasted 8 million years. By the end of it, the shape of the continents was as it is today. The fossils discovered in Pliocene soil show animal forms which are in many ways similar to those of the present. Other fossils belong to. species which are now extinct but it is easy to imagine the exact shape of their bodies.

The strangest of these were certain forms of proboscidea, such as the Amebolodon, with long, flexible noses.

Animal-life had already attained the variety of modern times when, about a million years ago, new changes in climate occurred, upsetting the pattern of life on the continents. The cold became intense and large ice-caps covered the globe as far down as our latitudes, driving nearly all the living beings towards the tropics.

Some animals, however, managed to adapt to the new climatic conditions and continued to live in the regions of the North. A typical example of this is the mammoth, a large woolly elephant, remains of which have even recently been found in the frozen sands of Siberia.

The severe cold froze vast stretches of water, particularly around the North and South Poles. Water vapour froze in the clouds and fell as snow, covering the continents so thickly that it did not melt. This made the flow of the rivers dwindle so much that many of them disappeared and the seas were no longer fed as they used to be. Yet the oceans continued to evaporate, although the vapour did not return to them as rain. The level of the oceans thus gradually dropped and the floors of the seas were revealed. Even the deep trench of the Bering Strait was left dry, after several million years under water.

When America was joined to Asia

When the deep trench of land of the Bering Strait was left dry, the two continents found themselves joined together again, as they had been in earlier times. The animals then began to migrate in profusion across the 'bridge' of Bering, particularly in the direction of America.

This migration had disastrous results for American animal-life. The herbivora (grass-eating animals) had lived on the plains of South America, completely cut off from the rest of the world, for at least 75 million years. With no great enemies to struggle against, these animals had gradually become lazy and had reached gigantic proportions which made their movements slow.

When the ferocious carnivora (flesh-eaters) of the old continent arrived from the North along the Bering Strait and down the chain of Central America, a mass slaughter took place. Nearly all the prehistoric American herbivora, incapable of defending themselves, were destroyed by the stronger, more intelligent newcomers.

When the ice retreated

The effects of the Great Ice Age and the retreat of the ice made a deep impression on the surface of the Earth. As they moved slowly along, the glaciers eroded and scoured, digging out valleys and gradually stripping the walls of rocks.

The trails of waste they removed piled up at the base and sides of the glaciers, where it eventually formed huge hills of rock debris.

Vast deposits of rock waste, left behind by the glaciers, are to be found around lakes, such as the Italian Lake Maggiore and Lake Garda.

There is another, more important aspect of the retreat of the glaciers. The enormous quantities of water, collected on hill-tops in the form of snow, rushed down into the valleys as the temperature rose. There they formed raging

As the sea and rivers successively rose and fell in the Great Ice Age, river—terraces were created

torrents and rivers which swept away all that came in their path. The mountains were eroded away but, at the same time, vast heaps of debris built up in the valleys. This action was particularly strong in the Alps.

The Po River Basin, which had been covered by the sea up until then, was formed in the Quaternary Period (which covers the last 2 million years) by the loads of debris carried down into the valley by the rivers.

WHEN LIFE BEGAN

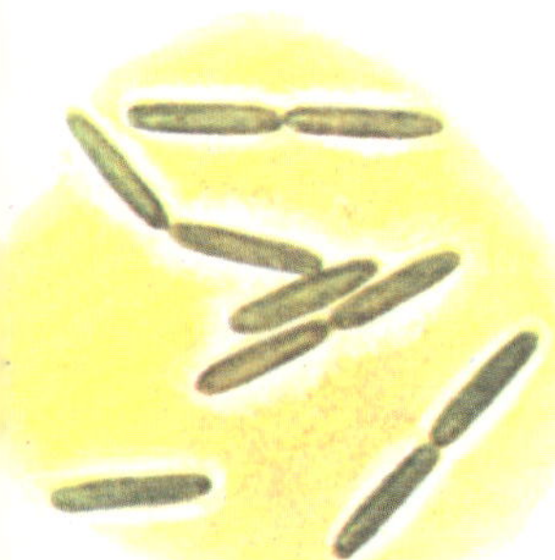

Pseudomonas fluorescens

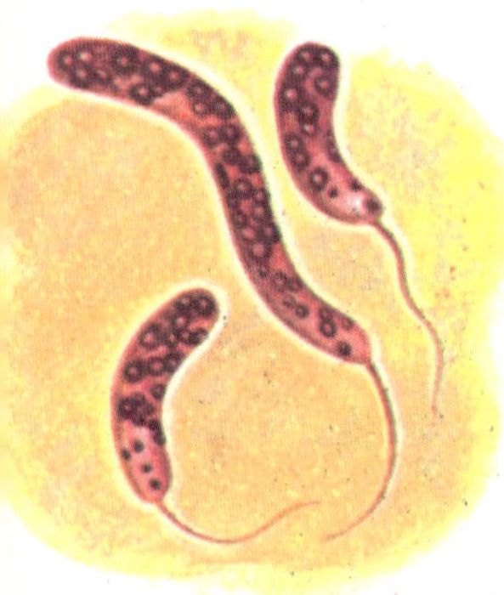

Thispirillum

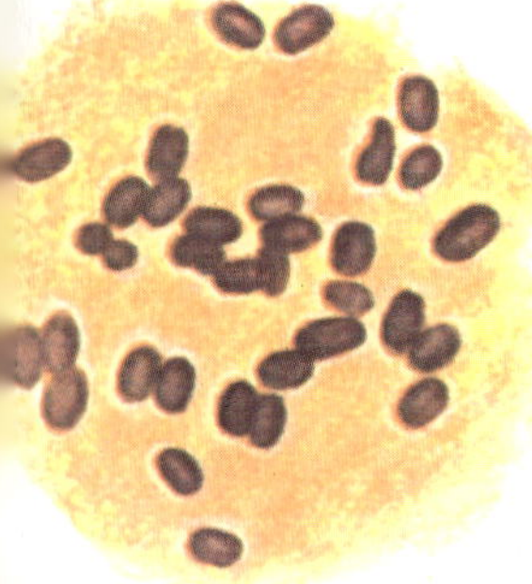

Nitrosomonas

The first plants did not grow on dry land but in the water. They were not proper plants but microscopic living beings which reproduced by splitting up. They gradually progressed through various stages of evolution until they became more complex beings, both animals and plants.

As these first living creatures (the flagellates) were so tiny and like jelly in consistency, they left no trace of their existence in the rocks. They have therefore given us no clues as to the exact period in which they appeared in the waters of the seas.

The oldest rocks, dating back to the dawn of life on Earth, have no traces of fossils in them at all. Scientists are nevertheless agreed that life must have begun on Earth about 3,000 million years ago and that it then evolved at a very slow rate.

The rocks belonging to the end of the Archaeozoic Era, which are therefore about 600 million years old, contain the first few fossil remains of blue-green algae, or sea-weed.

Although these remains are too scanty to enable us to make an exact reconstruction of the animal and plant life in those times, they are extremely important because they suggest that life must have begun long before that.

The algae were highly developed organisms compared with the primitive flagellates, and the gulf between these and the later living beings is tremendous.

According to the scientists, it took a very long time for the primitive little balls of jelly, half plant and half animal, to develop first into more advanced single-celled beings, distinctly either animals or plants, and then into beings with many cells.

The flagellates joined up at some point into colonies. They formed gelatinous masses of individuals, at first independent but then gradually more closely connected, until they became a single, more complex individual capable of reproducing, multiplying and dying.

It took nearly two and a half thousand million years of slow transformation for the very first living beings to reach such well-developed plant-forms as the algae.

The algae were, in fact, the first plants with well-defined vegetable characteristics to spread all over the globe but, of course, only where the surface was covered with water. The fossil imprints found on rocks formed 500 million years ago record the

The sequence from left to right illustrates how an area of bare ground can be colonized by a succession of plants

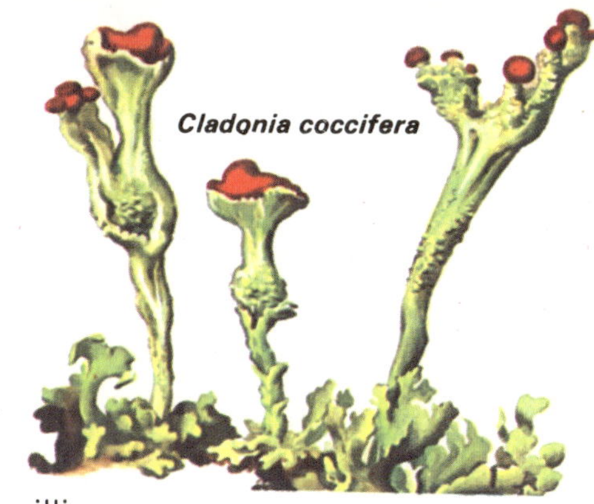

Cladonia coccifera

Thamnolia vermicularis

existence of a great variety of algae at the bottom of the sea, similar in every way to the modern sea-weed.

On dry land, however, there was still no trace of life, either animal or vegetable. The glare from the many volcanoes lit up a desolate landscape consisting solely of solidified lava, disintegrating rocks and huge mountains of sand and gravel washed up by the torrents of water.

When the algae left the water

About 435 million years ago, in the Silurian Period, a great upheaval in the crust of the Earth lifted the floors of many seas out of the water. This is probably what made the sea plants transform themselves, in order to survive. For hundreds of millions of years they had gone on vegetating in the water. When the basins dried up and they found themselves out in the air, they had to change their shape and organs in order to adapt to the new surroundings.

Once started, the evolution of the plants progressed rapidly. In little more than 150 million years the simple, almost microscopic algae became the gigantic trees which formed the immense forests of the Carboniferous Period.

To survive in the open air, the plants had to modify the organs on which they depended for life. The initial transformation was rather lengthy and we know little about it in detail but, as soon as the plants had acquired the ability to use the oxygen in the Earth's atmosphere, they found that conditions were perfect for developing new forms, more and more suited to their surroundings.

The bottom of the sea is always rich in the remains of plants and animals and these form quite a fertile soil. When large areas of land emerged from the sea as the waters retreated, they were therefore already covered with a thick layer of humus, or fertilizer, and could provide the plants with the ideal surroundings in which to develop. So the first land plants thrived and within 100 million years they had reached enormous proportions, forming the first forests.

These are some extinct varieties of horse-tail: (1) Shoot of *Calamophyton* (2) *Sphenophyllostachys* (3) *Crucicalamites* (4) *Protohyenia janovii*

When the first giant trees appeared

The first land plants evolved from the marine algae were fairly well developed but incapable of making seeds to reproduce themselves. To spread and perpetuate the species they used spores, as ferns and some other plants still do today. But, as with ferns, the spores, carried along by the wind, did not immediately grow into new plants when they fell to the ground. They only produced gametophytes—fine, heart-shaped blades which took root in the soil and there gave rise to egg-cells and male cells. From the union of these two cells the new plant was finally born.

For this complicated reproductive process to succeed, the spores needed very damp ground. As this type of plant can only spread in marshy regions and well-watered lowland, the ridges of the mountains and the drier places remained bare until plants capable of reproducing more rapidly appeared.

This new type of more complex plant evolved from another group of plants. They were the *Equiseta*, ferns and *Lycopodiales* which soon grew to gigantic proportions and covered the Earth with immense forests.

The *Lycopodiales* are known from rocks of the Silurian Period. Their remains form most of the great coal beds of the world. Today they exist in dwarf varieties such as club mosses, and are especially numerous in the tropics.

The *Equiseta*, or horse-tails, are particularly interesting because the last examples of this ancient plant are still growing around us, in uncultivated land and sandy soil, but in dwarf forms.

If we imagine horse-tails as big as trees, we will have some idea of how the forests looked 300 million years ago. The horse-tails are, in fact, the last descendants of the *Calamites*, plants which formed whole forests of horse-tails in prehistoric times. By a process of degeneration, or simplification, which is fairly common in the plant kingdom, these gigantic plants became smaller and smaller in the course of time, until they reached their present dwarf size.

About twenty-five species of horse-tail are known today, in every part of the world except southern Asia. They are found in a wide variety of habitats, sometimes in evergreen forms and sometimes in deciduous.

When the forests covered the Earth

The period following the formation of the continents and the trans-formation of the algae into land plants, enjoyed a climate which was particularly favourable for plant growth.

It was not too hot and the frequent rain created vast swamps which were ideal surroundings for the plants. Dense forests covered the ground. The humble little plants of earlier times had given way to other, more complex vegetation. Giant *Sigillaria*, about 23 metres high, tree-ferns, *Lycopodia* and other species grew up in a very short time. Their trunks, blown down by storms, piled up in thick layers of decaying wood. This happened between 300 and 250 million years ago. Later, the wood was to be covered by thick layers of mud and changed into coal.

We know from the coal we dig out of the bowels of the Earth that that is how it began. Not only have traces of the structure of the wood and stems of the plants been found in it but in the larger lumps signs of the life which dwelt in the ancient forests have appeared. As the tremendous natural forces reduced the trunks to shapeless layers of a heavy, black rock substance, so much of the life of those far-off times was wiped out, too.

The gingko, or maidenhair tree, is the sole survivor of a very ancient group of tree-plants. These trees are either male or female. They produce long shoots, giving rise to short spurs, on which male and female structures arise.

When the flowers appeared

The flower, from which fruit and seeds are derived, is the distinguishing feature of a more highly developed plant. It appeared only comparatively recently, about 100 million years ago.

Flowers therefore mark the last great stage in the evolution of the plant kingdom and developed almost at the same time as the appearance of the mammals. None of the plants which had formed extensive forests in the era before had proper flowers: gingkos (maidenhair trees), giant sequoias (gigantic conifers), poplars, oaks, willows and maples were the commonest varieties. Eventually, however, the first plants with obvious flowers appeared.

It was an extremely important event in the history of the Earth. The new species, helped by the swarms of pollinating insects which were already widespread, soon invaded all the land. They changed the look of the forests, creating a variety of living conditions which were very favourable to the new, warm-blooded little creatures which were quietly spreading to the four corners of the Earth. For many millions of years the primitive mammals remained hidden in the shade of these new plants, which grew into big forests. Then, one day, they began to invade the plains in profusion, too, giving rise to new species. The Cenozoic Era had begun.

When the animals appeared

Like plant-life, animal-life also began in the sea. It evolved from the earliest single-cell beings which lived in the water about 3,000 million years ago.

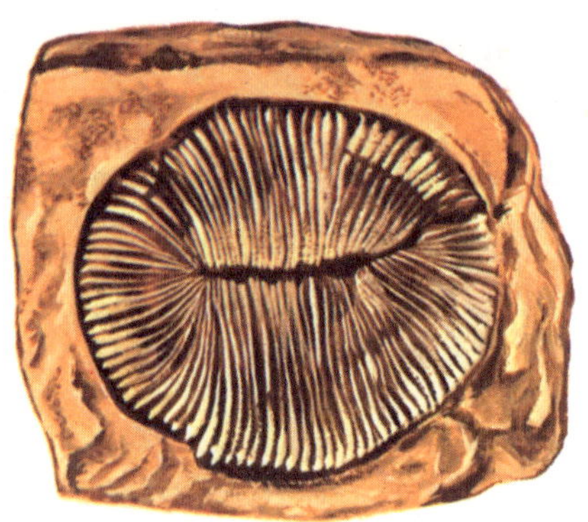

Fossil worms

This important moment in the history of life is marked by the appearance of the *Volvox*, a hollow, spherical flagellate which had a new, vital ability: it was capable of dying.

It may seem absurd, but the history of life on Earth really only began when death appeared. The *Volvox* was the first being capable of dying. Before it, the protozoa did not die but went on subdividing and reproducing over and over again. With the *Volvox* life had met the impassable limit of death.

From this important event in the history of living beings, the evolution of life became more and more complex and elaborate. Many millions of years after the appearance of the *Volvox*, colonies of sponges are to be found living at the bottom of the sea, decorating it with their strange shapes and gay colours.

They are colonies of tiny creatures called porifera, which share a common skeleton in the form of a hollow cone about 10 centimetres long, with the walls riddled with numerous pores. From dim, distant times to the present day the number of species of sponges living in the seas of the globe has multiplied but their basic structure has remained unaltered. Indeed the modern sponges are much the

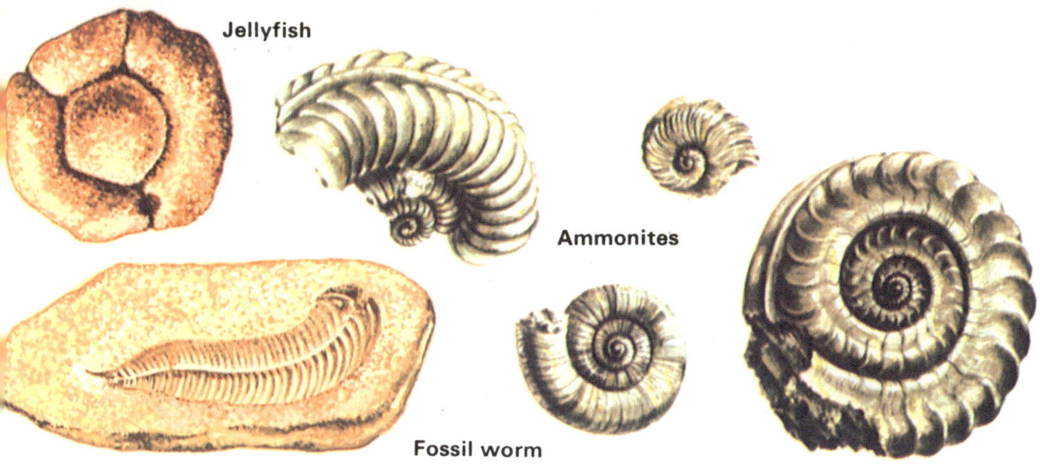

same as those which lived hundreds of millions of years ago, the fossil remains of which have been found in rocks going back as far as the start of the Palaeozoic Era.

Early naturalists regarded sponges as plants and it was not until the middle of the eighteenth century that the animal nature of sponges was recognized.

Sponges have long been common household items. In ancient Greece and Rome they were used for applying paint, as mops, and by soldiers as substitutes for drinking vessels.

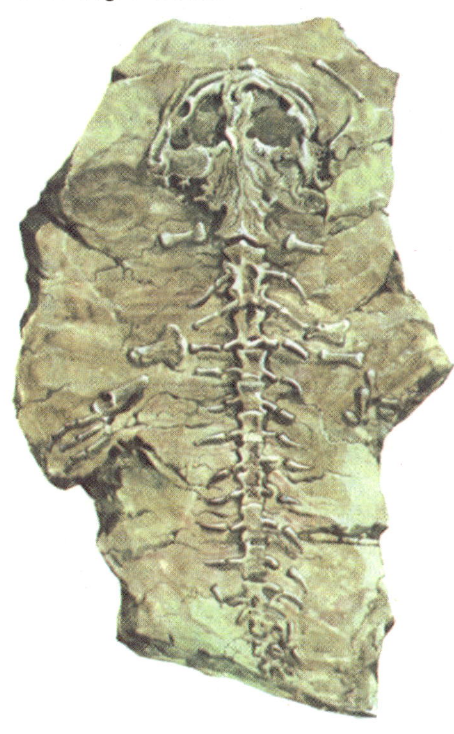

When the armoured animals appeared

After the sponges the first jellyfish and first octopus appeared. With these, evolution made another great step forward because, besides being animals with more than one cell, these creatures had a proper mouth and a proper stomach.

The first segmented worms and the first ring-worms, ancestors of the earth-worms and the insects, wriggled in the sand. The various parts of their bodies were already showing the first signs of specialization. There were many tiny flat-worms, too, with almost transparent bodies and no intestines but they are important because they already had the beginnings of a nervous system and a brain.

Life was being created at a steady pace and new, more complex orders of animals were developing. At the start of the Palaeozoic Era, the first animals capable of surrounding their bodies with protective armour appeared. They were little, odd-looking, crab-like creatures, equipped with various appendages. or legs, which helped them to swim or crawl on the bottom of the sea. The most widespread, because they reproduced the most, were the trilobites, ancestors of the modern crayfish, crabs and lobsters.

When the giant sea-snails were alive

The traces of fossil animals in the rocks of the Cambrian Period, dating back to 550 million years ago, confirm that the trilobites were some of the first animals to have armour to protect the soft parts of their bodies. As time passed, however, many other sea-dwellers learned how to produce limy shells.

Among these were huge giants nature evolved in an unexpected way. It appears that the first nautiloids had a very long, perfectly straight, cone-shaped shell but, as time passed, this folded back on itself, curling up in a spiral and becoming very like the shell of a snail.

The reason for this development is that it is easier to carry something rolled up than it is to drag the same weight on the ground. So the first nautiloids to be born with coiled shells had the advantage

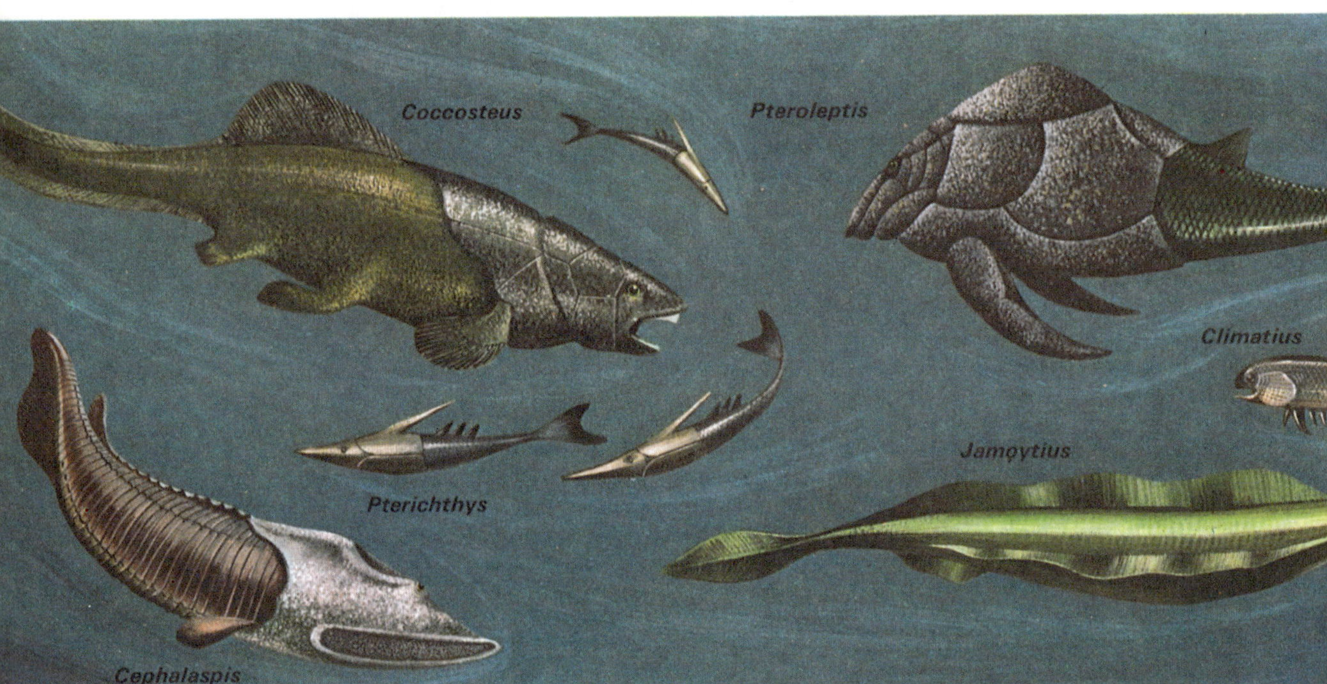

like the nautiloid, an enormous snail with tentacles. Its shell was shaped like a brightly coloured, elongated cone and grew up to 4 metres long. It was a predatory animal which crawled along the bottom of the sea, ready to snatch at its prey with long tentacles. The modern octopus and cuttle-fish were later evolved from it.

It is interesting to examine the fossils of nautiloids in rocks of different periods and see how over the others. The straight-shelled nautiloids gradually suc-combed to the hazards of their environment and disappeared, while the spiral-shelled ones spread more and more.

In rocks of the Silurian Period (430 million years ago) only fossils of nautiloids of the spiral-shell group are to be found, while traces of the long, conical shells have completely disappeared.

When animals with backbones appeared

The arrival of the vertebrates—animals with backbones—is important because it marks the start of the development of all the higher orders of animals, up as far as man. The vertebrates, too, first appeared in the sea.

The first being with a skeleton with a backbone was probably the *Ainiktozoon*, of which some fossil remains have been found. Its head was in one with its body and

The oldest traces of primitive fish forms date back to the mid-Ordovician Period. Fragments of bodies have been discovered in the Colorado and Wyoming districts. The most interesting of the fish illustrated here are the *Cephalaspis* (on the left) with a bony, flattened head-shield and a scaly body, and the torpedo-shaped *Jamoytius* with fin-like folds half-way down its sides.
The Coelacanth (on the right) is an example of a living fossil. It was discovered off East London, in South Africa, in 1938, proving that the Coelacanthids had survived for more than 70 million years. Since then, other similar specimens have been caught, telling us a great deal about them.

its backbone was fairly elementary. The first vertebrate fish which lived in the water were probably evolved from it.

They were armoured animals, without jaws, who rummaged in the mud at the bottom of the sea with their mouths wide open, looking for food. They quickly evolved into their present shapes, so that many fish which look much the same as the modern species are to be found in the

strata of the next periods.

When the *Ainiktozoon* appeared, the waters of the seas were brimming with life. Shellfish with shells in two parts, like the modern oyster, were already in existence and the primitive corals, which looked quite different from those of today and were more like transparent-petalled flowers, flourished. They lived and died on top of each other, piling their shells in huge layers. These were later transformed into rock from which mountains were formed.

When armoured fish lived in the sea

While the forests which gave rise to the coal seams were thriving on dry land, new species of vertebrate animals were developing in the sea.

The first fish, like the *Ainiktozoon*, were jawless so could not chew. With their mouths permanently gaping, they were only able to swallow tiny prey.

About 400 million years ago, however, new forms of fish, with jaws and teeth, made their appearance.

Their long heads were covered with a great many bony plates, decorated with small knobs, called tubercles. Their bodies, too, were protected at the front by a bony sheath, while the tail was free.

On the whole, these animals were tiny but there were also some which were gigantic, like the *Dinichthys*, which measured up to 6 metres long. There were also strange-shaped armoured fish similar to turtles and crabs, like the *Antiarcha*.

Fossil larvae of branchiosaurus, similar to salamanders

The amphibians had strong limbs and could move with equal agility on land and in the water

Later, unarmoured fish also appeared, which could breathe with both their gills and their lungs.

This ability proved extremely important, as it allowed some of these animals to leave the water from time to time, so becoming amphibious.

When the first land animals appeared

We have to wait until the Earth was invaded by the plants to find the first traces of animals capable of living out of the water. This is natural because the plant-eaters come before the meat-eaters in the chain of life. Without the plant-eaters the meat-eaters would have no food and, before the plant-eaters must come the plants, which are their essential food.

About 400 million years ago the Earth was covered with green. Even where the ground was rocky and barren, algae and lichens had managed to squeeze into the cracks, creating a base for the development of more advanced plants. The land was eventually ready to support the first animals and provide them with food and shelter. So they came.

We know for certain, although we do not know when, that they came from the water, leaving the bottom of the sea to venture on to dry land. The first land animals were probably scorpions, spiders, cockroaches and millepedes, all descendants of the sea-scorpion and all quite similar to the modern species.

The wings of the cockroaches were the first to beat in the air. Soon other little animals learned to fly. For the most part they were small insects which were quite different from the present ones, such as the six-winged *Steno-dictya*, fossils of which have come down to us preserved in clay and loam from the Carboniferous Period. The insects were often predators, who roamed the primeval forests, hunting for other little animals.

When the fish became amphibious

Over 350 million years ago, just before the great forests of the Carboniferous Period, some of the fish belonging to the primitive groups were born different from their ancestors. As well as gills, they found they had rudimentary lungs which allowed them to breathe the atmospheric air directly, instead of filtering the oxygen in the water through their gills. As a result, these fish could keep their heads out of the water for short spells, inhaling the air and passing it into their lungs.

One of these, darting in and out near the bank, was washed up on the dry beach by a sudden wave. Had it been a normal fish, it would have quickly died of suffocation, but its lungs helped it survive until it managed to crawl back into the water.

This was the vertebrate animals' first experience of a new, completely hostile environment, and the time spent out of the water was soon to prove invaluable.

These creatures were the ancient ancestors of the lung fish which are still found today in Australia, Africa and South America.

When the continents were raised again, many lakes dried up. Enormous numbers of fish died in the parched mud. Only the few fortunate species which were also provided with rudimentary lungs could survive. To keep alive, they dragged themselves laboriously along on their fins from puddle to puddle. Some, however, stayed on dry land, in the shade of the nearest bush, first for a short while then for longer and longer. This was probably the origin of the first amphibious animals, ideally suited to life on the marshy ground.

The amphibians who left the oldest fossil imprints on the rocks were the stegocephalians, who retained obvious signs of their close relationship with fish. We do not know if they still had traces of fins, but they definitely had a scaley cloak round their bodies, like fish. Sometimes, in some of the species, the scales thickened on their stomachs, knitting together to form a hard shell. This effective protection proved to be very useful when the stegocephalians crawled along the ground to get from place to place.

The development of these ancient animals and their gradual adaptation to new needs is an excellent illustration of the natural process of evolution.

Fossils of these first amphibians are to be found in rocks of the Devonian Period but there are many more in those of the Carboniferous and Permian worlds. The shape of their skulls, particularly their jaws, is strangely similar to that of the crossopterygian fish which, like the coelacanth, had stayed in the water.

Ranging from a few centimetres to many metres long, the stegocephalians came in a great variety of shapes. It was as if nature, after so long confined to the water, had at last exploded and was

Darwin was one of the first to put forward theories on the evolution of the species. They were explained in 1859 in his book, *On the Origin of Species by Means of Natural Selection*

enjoying suddenly creating a variety of different shapes from the same basic model.

These animals spent part of their lives on dry land and part in the water: the adjective 'amphibious' is therefore highly appropriate in their case, as it comes from a Greek word meaning 'leading two lives'. They crawled along the ground like the modern lizards, wandering among the trees and bushes of the ancient forests, hunting for insects and other little animals.

They never went far from the water's edge because they had not yet learned how to make hard-shelled eggs which could be laid straight on the ground, so they were compelled to return to the water when they were ready to reproduce. The young spent their early life there, perhaps because suitable food was more readily available in the water.

When the fish began to resemble modern varieties

In the days of the huge reptiles of 200 to 100 million years ago, life in the sea became very different. The armoured fish disappeared, perhaps destroyed by the voracious selachii, ancestors of the modern sharks.

The cartilaginous, or gristly fish (sharks, rays, chimaeras) whose skeletons are not made of bone but of a softer substance called cartilage, multiplied considerably and grew to enormous sizes. The bony fish then spread gradually, too, and branched out into a great variety of species.

They became widespread mainly because of the great skill they developed in swimming and obtaining food. By then they looked very much like their modern de-scendants.

Practically all the kinds of bony fish which inhabit the oceans today had already appeared about 100 million years ago and there has been little change in them since. There are more species of bony fish in the world than of any other vertebrate animal; 30,000 is probably an underestimate. They vary greatly in structure as well as in size and colour.

Nor have the giant turtles, which are fished in the sea today, changed since those days. Their origin is unknown but by the middle of the Triassic Period turtles were numerous. They are exactly the same now as the great *Archelon*, fossil imprints of which have been found in rocks 100 million years old.

The only sea-creatures to experience any new changes were the selachii. Many species disappeared, others were completely transformed until their scales looked like those of today.

When the Great Age of Reptiles began

Dinosaurs were gigantic reptiles which lived on the Earth in the Mesozoic Era for nearly 100 million years. They had evolved from the small amphibians who had so laboriously left the sea in the Devonian and Carboniferous Periods.

As soon as some of the amphibians learned how to produce hard-shelled eggs, they were able to do without the water where they had originally been compelled to lay their eggs. That was when the first reptiles were born and it happened about 300 million years ago, in the Carboniferous Period of the Palaeozoic Era.

The first reptile was probably the *Seymouria*, quite a small animal. A geological expedition in 1969 discovered that it had spread as far as the area which is now the South Pole. The most ancient reptiles also included the first giants, such as the *Moschops*, which was some 2 metres long.

The reptiles quickly multiplied all over the Earth, splitting up into numerous different groups. One of the most important was that of the small *Saltoposuchus*, the first reptile capable of walking on its hind-legs. From it, all the great dinosaurs were later evolved.

The tortoises and other small reptiles also made their appearance in this period. Their inconspicuous shapes would have passed unnoticed had not another extremely important group of animals—the lizards and snakes of today—been derived from them.

Some of the major groups of animals which have come down to the present day therefore have their forerunners in the start of the Mesozoic Era. Even the mammals have a direct ancestor in those far-off days. It was the *Cynognathus*, which was probably the first animal to have warm blood in its veins.

When the ancestor of the carnivorous dinosaurs appeared

When the reptiles appeared the Earth was bustling with activity. Each new reptile may be regarded as another experiment by Nature. Some of these experiments were successful and the new species developed, multiplied and stayed. Others failed and the new animals, ill-equipped to face the perils of their environment, gave way to their betters and the species became extinct.

Certainly one of Nature's most successful experiments at the start of the Mesozoic Era was the *Saltoposuchus.* It was only a small reptile, but it was very lively. It had also learned how to stand up and walk on its muscular, springy hind-legs which were perfect for sprinting. Its front legs, ending in strong, clawed fingers, were therefore free for grabbing at prey. So, in addition to its sharp, needle-shaped teeth, this reptile had two new offensive weapons. Indeed, it was so well equipped that, despite its size, the *Saltoposuchus* was not afraid to attack even very large prey, frequently getting the better of it.

Within a comparatively short space of time, all the dinosaurs had originated from this animal and, from the sub-branches, came all the modern birds and crocodiles.

When the largest reptiles became extinct

About 65 million years ago, almost without warning, the largest reptiles disappeared from the face of the Earth. The rock strata formed in later periods do not contain a single fossil of these animals. What brought about such an unexpected disappearance? How could the huge dinosaurs, who had dominated the Earth undisputed for nearly 100 million years, suddenly vanish without a trace?

Scientists have often tried to explain what happened, but none of their suggestions seems wholly convincing, although one theory has received more consideration than others. This is that the cause of the extinction of the dinosaurs was the collision of an asteroid with the Earth.

The evidence to support this conclusion lies in a thin layer of clay found in rocks throughout the world, which formed at the time when the dinosaurs disappeared. The clay is rich in the element iridium, a metal that is normally rare on Earth but fairly common in meteorites. It seems very likely that the iridium originated in an asteroid that collided with the Earth at that time.

The force of the collision would have created a world-wide cloud of iridium-rich dust that eventually fell to the ground to form the layer of clay. However, in the meantime, the cloud would have cut off sunlight, and this would result in a long period of intense cold during which the dinosaurs would have either frozen to death or died of starvation.

When the reptiles flew

Perhaps we shall never know for what mysterious reasons some of the reptiles suddenly tried to take to the air and conquer the sky. The fact is, however, that traces of numerous winged reptiles are to be found next to the fossils of the great dinosaurs dating from more than 130 million years ago.

One of the most widespread and the most ancient was the *Dimorphodon*. It looked like a monstrous bat and its size was remarkable: its skull alone measured 22 centimetres long.

The large-skulled *Dimorphodons* disappeared quickly, to be followed by other winged reptiles of various shapes and sizes. The *Rhamphorhynchus* was very common, with its peculiar tail ending in a diamond-shaped rudder, and there were various pterodactyls. The name means 'winged fingers' and refers to the very long little finger which kept the whole flap of flying-membrane taut.

In the course of time the winged reptiles grew bigger and bigger and better and better at flying. The largest and the best at flying was probably the *Pteranodon,* fossils of which have been found in North America and Russia.

It had a wing span of a good 7 metres and spent its time skimming over the water, catching fish and shellfish. Its incredibly wide wings prevented it from walking comfortably so, on the ground, it was probably compelled to crawl on its stomach but, in the air, with its light weight of only 12 kilos, it was amazingly agile.

Like the land dinosaurs, the winged reptiles, too, disappeared from our globe almost without warning, about 65 million years ago. The reason for their sudden extinction still remains a mystery.

Diatryma (above)

Phororhachus (below)

When the ancestors of the birds appeared

Strange as it may seem, the first birds did not evolve from the winged reptiles. Their forerunner was certainly a reptile but a different kind from that of the flying *Sauria*. The first of these creatures to leave us a clear picture on the rocks was the *Archaeopteryx*, which lived with the great dinosaurs over 130 million years ago.

The fossil imprints of this primitive bird are so complete that they tell us exactly what it looked like.

About as big as a pigeon, it was a strange mixture of half bird and half reptile. Obvious signs of its close relationship with reptiles are the movable, clawed fingers on its wings, its tail of twenty individual joints and its toothed jaw. Yet its body was covered with a fringe of feathers, which was something completely new.

Its wings were no longer a sheet of skin but a fan of feathers which spread out and beat the air as it flew. It was still a very simple flying machine, in need of a great many improvements and, indeed, the *Archaeopteryx* was a poor flyer, but its appearance marked an important stage in the history of evolution.

The first bird was definitely not a predator because its jaws were too weak. Perhaps it only fed on fruit, berries and small larvae. To take off, it clambered up to the top of a tree and launched itself out into space.

After this first laborious performance, the birds multiplied rapidly. Their ability to fly improved and they became the only true lords of the sky.

There was a time, in the evolution of the animals, when the fiercest predators of the plains were not mammals but enormous birds with savage beaks. They could not fly but ran with great speed. All derived from the primitive *Archaeopteryx*, they soon increased in number, sometimes reaching gigantic proportions, and competed for the hunting field with the carnivorous mammals.

When the giant birds appeared

About 70 million years ago, on the plains of South America, lived the *Onactornis*, a giant running bird nearly 3 metres tall.

It had a very strong, hooked beak nearly 40 centimetres long. Fierce and cruel by nature, it, too, swooped down on the large mammals of the plains, trying to tear their stomachs open to make them bleed to death and so provide itself with a plentiful supply of food.

Many other meat-eating birds lived at that time and were equally fierce and dangerous, although smaller in stature. Some lived until comparatively recently, like the legendary *Aepyornis.* Skeletons discovered in the swamps of Madagascar show that this was an enormous bird, 3 metres tall, weighing some 500 kilos, which walked on two strong runner's legs.

According to the tales of some early travellers, this bird was still living in Madagascar a few centuries ago, particularly in the swampy regions of the south, and it only disappeared quite recently.

When the first mammals appeared

The appearance of the first mammals on the Earth went almost unnoticed, at the time when the dinosaurs were at their peak. Strange new animals, small but very active and much more intelligent than the dinosaurs, gradually came to live in the forests and glades. Unlike the reptiles, they were warm-blooded and therefore not affected by climatic changes. Continually circulating through their bodies, their blood kept their body temperature at a constant heat. This suddenly proved to be extremely important because it allowed the new creatures to cope with seasonal changes in climate without being affected by them too much. These changes became more and more noticeable towards the end of the Era and eventually made the great dinosaurs disappear.

Another feature of the new animals was a more highly developed maternal instinct, which

Early examples of plant-eaters: the *Phenacodus* (below) had small hooves but its skull and teeth were ill-suited for grazing; the *Coryphodon* (centre) was bigger and had longer teeth; the biggest was the *Uintatherium* (above) which had bony bulges on the top of its skull which must have made it look rather odd.

led them to look after their young, while the dinosaurs could not care less, once they had laid their eggs. The young of the warm-blooded animals were born alive and nursed by their mothers until they were ready to eat other food. This, too, is a very important characteristic and one of the mammals' most distinguishing features. In fact, they are called mammals because they have the mammae, or milk glands, with which they feed their young.

We know very little of the first mammals who dwelt in the forests at the time of the last dinosaurs because their fossil remains are rather scarce. Certainly one of the most ancient was the *Morganucodon,* which lived about 160 million years ago, in the Great Age of Reptiles. It measured 10 centimetres long and had a remarkable resemblance to the modern shrew-mouse. Other ancient mammals were the *Prodiacon,* a primitive hedgehog, and the *Taeniolabis,* one of the first to feed on plants. The others ate mainly insects, slugs and snails.

Homo habilis:
skull-cap and jaw

When the giant mammals were alive

At the same time as the dinosaurs disappeared, about 65 million years ago, the mammals made a great advance. Numerous branches developed from the primitive stock of mostly small rodents and became carnivores or herbivores. The herbivores, or grass-eaters, quickly multiplied and in 10 million years had greatly increased in size and were much bigger than the modern sheep.

Some of the most interesting grass-eaters of the period were the *Pantolambda,* 115 centimetres long, and the *Barylambda,* almost 3 metres long. Both of them were already provided with hooves at the end of their legs, like their modern descendants.

With the plentiful food and the pleasant climate, the grass-eaters grew to be gigantic. Proof of this are the fossil remains of the *Baluchitherium,* a huge rhinoceros of the Oligocene Period, without doubt the largest land mammal which ever existed. It was five and a half metres high and rested on four enormous legs like tree-trunks. The first fossils of this animal were found in Baluchistan at the beginning of this century.

In strata of earth formed 38 million years ago, there are also many fossils of the *Brontotherium,* a group of grass-eating animals some 4 metres long.

Perhaps these animals were crushed by their own weight. They became weaker and weaker and finally disappeared, to be replaced by more agile, stronger types. Cases such as this are frequently met with in the evolution of animals, when over-specialization leads to the extinction of a species.

When the first mammoth was discovered

The mammoth is not a true fore-runner of the present-day elephant. Both derive from the same older ancestor.

The mammoth lived in the Quaternary Era and was therefore a contemporary of the first men. Complete examples of this animal, which disappeared tens of thousands of years ago, have been found, perfectly preserved, in the frozen ground of Siberia.

The first discovery of a frozen mammoth was made in Berezovka, in Siberia, in 1899. This was one of the most complete mammoth carcases ever discovered. Perhaps it had fallen into a deep crevasse in the ice, because its right fore-leg and the bottom of its back were broken.

As it fell, the mammoth triggered off an avalanche of snow which covered it, wedging it in a grip of ice. For many centuries it stayed buried there like that, until the ice melted. Its body then began to decompose and the foul smell attracted the attention of some passing fur-trappers' dogs.

When the first experts arrived they found that the hair, the skin and even the blood of the mammoth had been perfectly preserved.

Since then, many other bodies of mammoths have been discovered intact in the ice. These discoveries have told us all about the great proboscids with their huge curving tusks which lived in the Great Ice Age but which were very different from the modern African and Indian elephants.

Many stuffed mammoths are to be seen in museums today.

When the hominids made their appearance on the Earth

The Neozoic Era is usually divided into two periods: the Pleistocene, which included the Great Ice Age, and the Holocene, which saw man assert himself over all other creatures in Creation. According to most geologists, traces of the first men date back to the start of this era, although there are some who claim that a primeval species of human being was already in existence at the end of the previous era. During the whole of the Pleistocene Period man spread very slowly over the Earth. With only his physical strength to help him, he had to fight for survival against difficulties and dangers of every kind.

The worst danger lay in the fierce, great animals with which primitive man had to battle for control of the woods and plains. Many of these animals, like the sabre-toothed tiger and the cave-bear, disappeared long ago; others, like the lion, the hyena and the leopard, retreated from our regions

The hominids, as they are called, were very different from *Homo sapiens*, our ancestor

in historical times but still live today in hotter, more congenial climates.

The mammoth still lived in the colder regions and was certainly stalked by the first tribes of huntsmen. A slaughtered mammoth meant an enormous supply of meat for the whole tribe, so the primitive hunters devised ingenious traps to catch these huge beasts. For in their fight with the mammoth and the other terrible wild animals which threatened them, their most effective weapon was their intelligence.

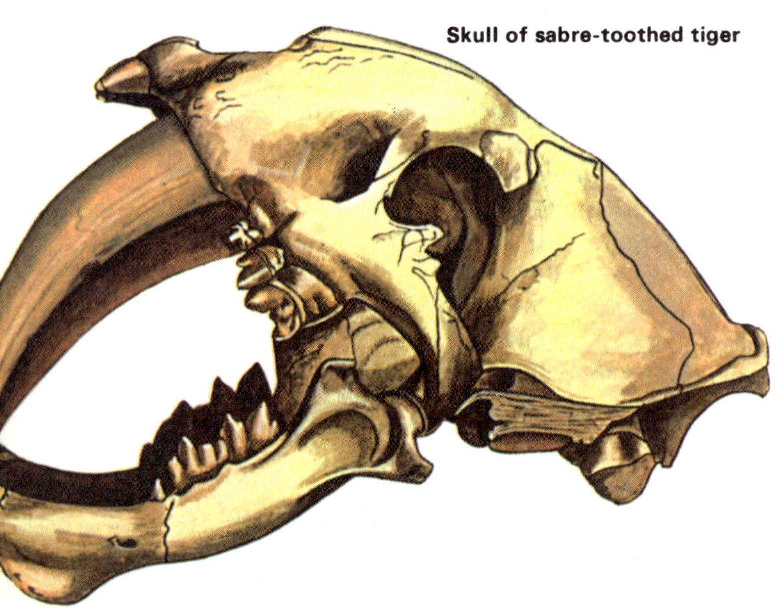

Skull of sabre-toothed tiger

Where had this new creature come from, who was patiently extending his dominion over all the other animals? By which evolutionary process was he born? The answer is easy, yet very difficult. Although many fossils point to the direct evolution of man from more primitive beings, themselves evolved from certain families of apes, the same fossils cannot explain how, at a certain moment in the history of evolution, a miraculous spark of intelligence was kindled in the brains of our ancestors.

In the development of animal life, the most surprising discoveries have been about the evolution of the apes. They, too, appeared in dim, distant times and then gradually split up into different groups, some of which looked quite like man.

Numerous fossil discoveries made in the last decades have shown that some extinct branches of the family of apes had learned not only how to walk upright, like man, but how to make and use primitive tools. In particular, they had rough weapons for fighting their opponents. These were the hominids—animals of the family of man—but they were still very different from *Homo sapiens,* who was our direct ancestor.

According to the most recent discoveries, the hominids lived between the end of the Tertiary Era and the start of the Quaternary. At one time it was thought that human life was only 600,000 years old but now many scientists are inclined to think that we must go back about 3.5 million years ago to find the early hominids.

Throughout the Quaternary Era subman continued to progress, going through various stages which are recorded by fossil discoveries of skulls and other parts of the skeleton.

These discoveries mark steps in the evolution of mankind. The earliest known hominids, which have a large brain and walked on two legs, lived in Tanzania about 3.5 million years ago. They were called *Australopithecus.* Later hominids include *Homo habilis*, dating back 2 million years in Kenya, and *Homo erectus*, who lived in Kenya 1.5 million years ago.

When Neanderthal Man appeared

Pithecanthropus (*or Homo erectus*) was already able to make simple stone tools. His favourite weapon was a large stone chipped into an oval shape like a large almond, which he clutched in both hands or tied to a stick, so making the first axe.

A variation of this subman was *Sinanthropus*, or Chinese Man, who had an even more developed skull and whose fossil remains date back to 500,000 years ago.

Over 400,000 years then passed before the appearance of Neanderthal Man, the creature who finally gave up the wandering life and a diet of plants, slugs and snails to become a hunter, starting to eat the meat of his prey.

He takes his name from the Neanderthal Valley, near Düsseldorf in Germany. There, in 1856, in a small cave, the first fossil remains of a new race of human beings, far more complex than *Pithecanthropus*, were discovered. There was only the top of a skull and a few bones but soon many other discoveries were being made in various parts of Europe—in France, in Belgium, in Gibraltar and in Yugoslavia—and so it was possible to understand the habits of these men, who already knew how to work flints with great skill.

Neanderthal Man was quite small. His average height was only 1·55 metres but his body was broad and his muscles were strong. He had an ape-like skull, with heavy, arched eyebrow-ridges which met in the middle. His face was long with wide cheekbones and a broad, flat nose.

His forehead and chin were receding, and he had a short neck.

With his hairy body and ape-like face he looked brutish and savage. Yet his brain was as big as that of modern man. Neanderthal Man already possessed a remarkable degree of intelligence, which we can tell by the artistic workmanship which he put into making numerous objects from wood, bone and flint.

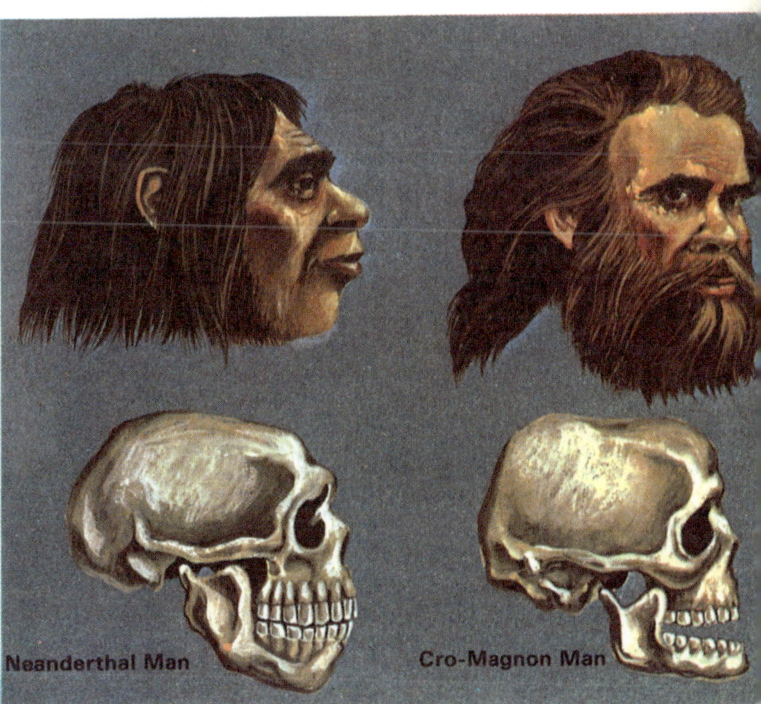

When man lived in caves

The Neanderthal family of men lived when the ice of the Quaternary Era was at its most extensive. They were therefore for the most part cave-dwellers, for it was only in caves that they could find proper shelter from the severe cold.

They were clever hunters and banded together in groups to catch the rhinoceros, bisons, reindeer and goats which lived around them. In this they were experiencing the first forms of social contact.

They still did not know how to make fire so ate mostly raw meat, to which they seem to have added a little clay, although it is not clear why. Certainly this habit of chewing meat mixed with clay quickly wore away the enamel of their teeth, which decayed, hurt and soon fell out. Judging by the skulls discovered, toothache was the most common illness among the men of this race.

The most developed worked their flints with amazing speed, making a very varied selection of tools.

They buried their dead. Scraps of food and flint objects which they would have used in their daily lives have been found in their graves, next to the dead person, as if he might need them in a future life.

Details like this suggest that these primitive people believed in a life after death, which means that their religious beliefs and customs must have been quite advanced. Yet there is no connection between these customs and those of the men who lived nearer us in time, because this last group belongs to a family which has nothing to do with that of Neanderthal Man.

The caves in which early man dwelt are full of the fossil remains of enormous beasts who occupied them in competition with our ancient forefathers. The remains are often skeletons of the cave-bear, the direct ancestor of our brown bear, which it closely resembles.

This animal was much bigger than the modern bears, however. It had a bigger head with a bulging forehead and strong fangs, and shorter legs. Usually, anyone who wanted to make his home in a cave had first to drive out the bear, smoking it out with a bonfire at the entrance and then attacking it with his primitive stone weapons. Once taken, the cave then had to be defended against the nightly invasions of the wild animals, so fires were lit around the entrance.

Skeletons of cave-bears have been found in European caves and more than 800 were found in one cave alone in France. In some cases their skulls were smashed in, which is an obvious sign that man had engaged the beasts in a fierce fight and had won.

Other fearful animals with which primitive man had to struggle were the sabre-toothed tiger, which had excessively long fangs, as the name suggests, the lion, the leopard, the cave-hyena, the wild ox, the hippopotamus and the rhinoceros. It was certainly an unfair fight but the feeble little men, with no useful natural defences, often got the better of these wild beasts, thanks to their cunning.

When the first forms of civilization were born

We belong to the family of *Homo sapiens*, or thinking man, who succeeded in coming to the fore about 40,000 years ago but who is not directly descended from the Neanderthals. There is a great gap between the two branches of humans which science has not yet managed to bridge. We do not know where *Homo sapiens* came from. We only know that at some point, in the most recent strata, there appeared skeletons of highly developed men, just like the modern races.

The most important discovery, as far as *Homo sapiens* is concerned, was made in 1868. That year, during excavations for a railway line at Cro-Magnon, a village in the Dordogne, in France, an ancient grave was found with five incomplete but recognizable human skeletons, together with animal bones, sea shells made into necklaces and stone tools.

These skeletons belonged to some muscular, very tall men, on average 1·87 metres, with skulls very similar to ours, although still with heavy eyebrow-ridges. They had large brains and broad, short faces with narrow mouths. After that, skeletons similar to those of Cro-Magnon were discovered in nearly every part of Europe.

The graves of these ancient men already show the first signs of civilization.

Cro-Magnon Man was the first to create works of art, to learn how to cultivate the fields and raise animals, to discover metals. These men were the founders of the first ancient civilizations.

In the cave of Le Madeleine in France there were discovered some very interesting remains from the later Palaeolithic Period. The stone implements of the Magdalenians are of no great value but they were masters at working with bone.

Among various Magdalenian bone implements are harpoons, javelins, eyed needles and chisels.

The Magdalenian culture of advanced Palaeolithic Man has much in common with Eskimo culture. These peoples had similar survival problems, and they solved them in similar ways.

But the most remarkable testimony left to us of our prehistoric ancestors is not so much their implements as their sculptures and paintings. What has remained is often of great beauty—wall inscriptions, paintings, animal sculptures, and statuettes of female figures made of mammoth ivory and fine grained rock.

It is difficult to understand what inspired the creation of these works of art. They may have been part of a magic ritual intended to bring success in hunting.

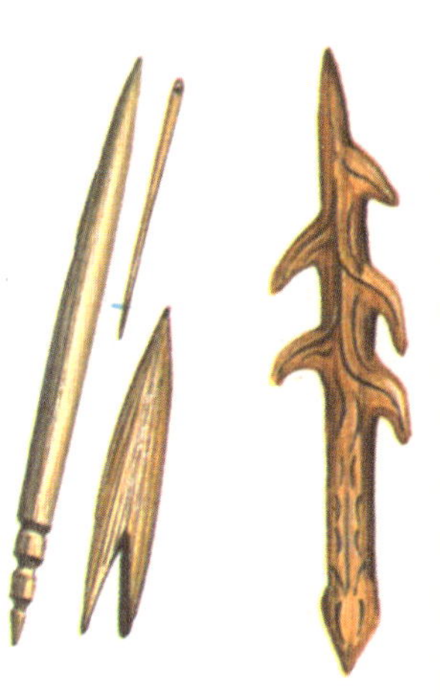

WHEN CIVILIZATION BEGAN

The people who lived thousands of years before us left many traces of their existence. They are mostly objects of every day use, such as charms, weapons, tools, coins or even ruins of their homes, all revealing the history of the people.

Archaeology is the science which tries to collect enough information from the remains of the ancient peoples to find out how they lived.

The work is extremely difficult because it requires both enthusiasm and patience, inspiration and method. Very rarely does the archaeologist have the good fortune to come across particularly valuable and significant remains and his work seldom makes the front-page story.

It is more a labour of love, painstaking determination and perseverance which hardly ever fire the imagination of the general public.

The archaeologist loves beautiful things of the past. He is an enthusiast who finds his work sufficiently rewarding to make up for its difficulties. For archaeology is a science which needs dedication and great perseverance.

When archaeology began

The enthusiasm which inspired the scholars of the Renaissance during the fourteenth, fifteenth and sixteenth centuries, and their love for anything to do with classical Greek and Roman art, led to the first archaeological excavations. The lack of any precise methods of research and adequate scientific means was compensated for by the eagerness of the excited diggers.

The results, however, were of little importance. Anything which was brought to light nearly always ended up in the noble mansions of whoever had financed the excavations. They thus came to form the first great private collections of archaeological treasures, which can still be admired today.

Renaissance archaeology was not therefore supported by any notable follow-up. It was only towards the middle of the eighteenth century that an interest in the past was awakened in the world of Western culture. For example, the discovery of Herculaneum, buried by the famous eruption of Vesuvius on 24 August A.D. 79 was started in 1709.

Any sensible, well-organized methods of excavation were still a long way off, however. The men employed to do the actual digging were often so clumsy that they seriously damaged the works of art they were uncovering.

The archaeologists who worked in the second half of the eighteenth century and the whole of the nineteenth may be regarded as the true pioneers. Their enthusiasm filled the obvious gaps in their preparation.

The most important were Winckelmann, Schliemann and Pitt Rivers.

After them came a second generation of archaeologists, better prepared both from the educational and the archaeological point of view. The most famous of these were the Frenchman, Henri Breuil, the Englishman, L. S. B. Leakey, and the Chinaman, Pei-Wen-Chung. With them archaeology became a true science.

The science of archaeology employs some extremely complicated techniques which require highly specialized knowledge. Today archaeologists have to be scientists, teachers and organizers. Sir Mortimer Wheeler, R. Braidwood and R. Heizer are forerunners of this type of archeologist. The work is done under the closest supervision, with almost mathematical precision. Many features of the pioneer days of archaeology have changed but the modern scientists reveal the same enthusiasm which has been the solution to so many problems.

But archaeology is not concerned only with buried treasures from lost cities. Archaeologists often spend most of their time on simple objects of daily use.

L. S. B. Leakey (above)
Sir Mortimer Wheeler (below)

Below:
A. Pitt Rivers (left),
H. Schliemann (centre)
H. Breuil (right)

When man learned how to use stone

The appearance of *Homo sapiens*, or thinking man, on the Earth is said by the experts to date back to somewhere around 100,000 years ago.

This period is also known as the Palaeolithic Age, which means the Old Stone Age. The name refers to the numerous findings, all over the world, of pointed stones which primitive man learned to make into weapons and tools.

He used thin pieces of flints as a rule, pointing and sharpening them at the edges by patiently striking them with harder stones. These flakes could be shaped into a kind of knife. Skilful craftsmen could probably produce them quickly when they were needed.

Archaeological excavations have unearthed an incalculable number of these weapons in various shapes and sizes, but all clearly from the same source: hand-made by man.

When the first works of art were created

Primitive man evolved slowly. In the Upper Palaeolithic Age, or towards the end of the Old Stone Age, about 10,000 years ago, the first works of art are to be found. There are paintings, engravings and carvings made from a variety of materials, such as bone, clay and stone itself.

The sculptures which modern archaeology has unearthed are often astonishingly perfect and show great artistic skill. Considering the period in which they were made, some of them are quite extraordinary, as, for example, the ivory sculptures portraying a human figure.

The models frequently glorify fertility, bearer of peace and plenty, depicted in statuettes as a woman expecting a child.

His use of different materials to express himself reflects a remarkable cultural advance in Upper Palaeolithic Man.

When the first rock-paintings were made

The Stone Age cave paintings and engravings are true works of art. Some of them have only been discovered quite recently.

They are mostly pictures of large animals hunted or particularly admired by primitive man. Scholars have studied them carefully and have noticed how well those primitive artists were able to express the drama of a scene.

An example of this is the way in which the animals were frequently out of proportion to the men: the exaggerated hugeness of a mammoth is a sign of the feeling of inferiority which man often had, particularly during a hunt.

The use of bold shades of colour helps to heighten the effect and the realism of the primitive paintings. Yet the true meaning of ancient art still puzzles archaeologists and scholars today.

When man learned how to make earthenware pots

Archaeologists, who know how to reconstruct the history of man from the relics he leaves in the ground, call the period in which man learned how to make polished stone tools the Neolithic Age, or the New Stone Age. It lasted from about 8000 to 5000 B.C.

Towards 6500 B.C. man began to make earthenware pots. This new skill was extremely important, firstly because of the practical usefulness of crockery in the lives of the people, who had by then become animal and crop farmers; and secondly because making pots encouraged the craftsmen to try other forms of art.

Beautifully made pots from the Neolithic Age are proof that man was rapidly approaching quite an advanced state of civilization. Soon wood, leather and then metal were being used to make pots, as well as earthenware.

When Archaeology became a comparative science

Archaeological investigations often used to specialize in the old days by going deeply into the discoveries they had dug up and so reconstructing the life of a people. This type of specialization has today been replaced by a more modern approach, which involves the comparative study of the discoveries.

What is 'comparative archaeology'? For example, the primitive dwellings so far discovered all over the world and belonging to a particular period are studied in detail. The results of this research are compared and provide useful pointers for understanding the people and the different aspects of their lives: society, trade, art and so on.

So the archaeologist today is no longer an inspired detective with a clever knack of uncovering clues to the past, but a painstaking scientist ready to work with other scholars to achieve a common aim. We must hope that the archaeologist of the twenty-first century will have the widest back-up support: skilled workers, technicians, photographers, recording staff, helicopters for checking localities, laboratories (mobile, permanent and central) for the analysis of remains found during excavations.

When the first boats appeared

One of the most fascinating archaeological trails is that left by boats. Who were the first people brave enough to launch boats capable of making trips along the coast?

Our evidence shows that the people of the island of Crete were the first navigators of the sea. This achievement is thought to have been made in the Neolithic Age. It is known for certain that by 3000 B.C. the inhabitants of Crete were expert seamen and were travelling to and from Egypt. There they sold their cargoes, which were mostly of obsidian, a black, glossy volcanic flint, which was in great demand for making sharp tools and weapons.

The Cretans even ventured as far as the Lipari Islands to stock up with materials which were in short supply on their own island.

Gallery grave at New Grange, Ireland. In these monuments there is a gallery or chamber built of stone slabs, sometimes with several compartments.

When the first villages grew up

In the Near East, roughly where Palestine is now, recent archaeological investigations have unearthed the rich remains of a Neolithic civilization which flourished 9,000 years before Christ.

The structure of the houses is remarkably advanced. Both the outside and inside walls are built of stone and each room in the house is separate. Although the roofs are thatched they are supported by solid rafters.

Even the furnishings, ovens, stone pots and mats are evidence of a civilized culture. The houses are not isolated but grouped together in villages of about fifty dwellings each.

When evidence of megalithic culture occurred

At one time it was thought that megalithic (or huge stone) monuments belonged to a particular culture which was especially widespread in Europe. Later discoveries have shown that the use of vast stones, some of them really colossal, was common to the primitive peoples all over the world.

There are many kinds of megalithic monument, from the megaliths of Japan to those of Holland, from the stone heads of Easter Island or Spain to those of India, from the carved blocks found in Ireland at the entrance to enormous graves to the the tombstones still in use by the African peoples.

Some particularly interesting examples of megalithic monuments are the gallery graves to be found in the west of England and Ireland.

An Australian limekiln (above); Medieval markings on brick (below); Inca wall (right)

One of the most fascinating archaeological trails is that left by boats. The photograph shows an ivory model of a boat, discovered at Knossos, Crete.

Neolithic house at Hacilar, Asia Minor

When the Neolithic Age developed in Europe

The archaeologist has to explain many problems, for the discoveries he makes with such patience are not always easy to interpret.

A mound in which several pots have been stacked, for example, might have been a tomb or it could really have been a shop or a store. Signs of burning could mean houses, places of worship or public places where skins were smoked. Even some large monuments and complicated architectural constructions are sometimes so puzzling as to remain unexplained. This is the case of Stonehenge, in Wiltshire.

It consists of large circles, approached down a long avenue. Seen from above they look like a giant keyhole. The whole area is bounded by a low, unfortified bank with all the houses on the outside. The most complex structure is in the middle. It comprises a circular colonnade of enormous stone uprights with lintels, also of stone, linking the ring of uprights. Inside this a second row of twin posts, again linked by lintels, dominates the structure which altogether seems like a temple or a place kept for funeral ceremonies.

Archaeologists are still uncertain why it was built, although they are inclined to believe it was used for religious, perhaps astronomical, purposes – possibly even to predict eclipses. Stonehenge was built over several centuries, the first phase of construction occurring in about 2100 BC.

Henges are common throughout Europe and date back to the end of the Stone Age and up to the Bronze Age.

When the Neolithic Age ended in Europe

Archaeological discoveries are sometimes amazing, like the discovery of some beakers, apparently commonplace objects, called bell beakers because of their shape.

The people who made these beakers in their millions, all more or less alike although with different decorations, spread over much of Europe at the end of the Stone Age. They were the same people who built the great henges.

Traces of these people have been found in eastern Europe in Czechoslavakia and Hungary, and in western Europe in England, Spain and Sicily. Many bell beakers have been found in tombs, together with ornaments of gold, amber, jet, a greenish-blue stone, probably turquoise, and flint and

Stonehenge in Wiltshire consists of large circles, approached down a long avenue (left)

Neolithic objects from England: copper daggers, flints and pitchers (above and below)

53

Two-handled jar of pale green Lung Ch'uan celadon

copper weapons: daggers, arrow tips and spears.

The origin of these beakers and the way in which they were made are still subjects for discussion among the experts. Some say they originated from Spain, others from Holland, others again claim the influence of the area which now corresponds to France.

One fact, however, is clear: the prehistoric people who made them had a great influence on European civilization, throwing it into such a state of activity that it quickly progressed towards a more advanced way of life.

Their importance becomes all the greater if we remember that the ancient civilizations of the Near East, such as the Egyptian, were already flourishing. So, on this side of the Mediterranean, the Stone Age was still acting as a brake on more advanced forms of culture. The people of the henges and the bell beakers took Europe into the Bronze Age about 1,000 years behind the times.

When the Mesolithic Age flourished

Historians separate the Palaeolithic from the Neolithic by another age which they call the Mesolithic. Mesolithic culture did not appear among all the peoples of the times but its special features are evident in some of them.

One distinction of the Mesolithic Age was a marked improvement in hunting and grain harvesting methods. The biggest animals had died out after the last cold spell. The smaller game was extremely plentiful but even more difficult to catch than its predecessors. If the mammoth had presented hunting problems because of its enormous size, the deer, wild boar, fish and birds proved to be in some ways more difficult prey because they were more agile and cunning.

Mesolithic Man knew how to invent baited traps for the fish and snares, bows and arrows for catching animals. Two separate archaeological excavations, one in Europe and one in Asia, are particularly enlightening about the life of the men who lived in the Mesolithic Age. At Star Carr in Yorkshire flake tools, scrapers, harpoon and lance heads made from red deer horn have been unearthed and a wooden canoe paddle has been found intact.

At Belt in Iran examples of different stages of Mesolithic culture, dating from 9500 B.C. to 6600 B.C. were found in one single cave. The relics left by the ancient inhabitants of this cave show how their activities progressed: bows and arrows for catching seals from the earliest occupants, weapons for catching gazelles from the next.

Ko dish netted with a fine crackle (above)

Ju dish with petal foot (below)

When the Neolithic Age flourished

The Neolithic Age is usually known as the New Stone Age, referring to stone which man had polished. Yet historians and archaeologists agree that the two most important features of this period are the transformation of man from a hunter to a breeder and from a gatherer to a cultivator.

It was in this period, that man learned how to take care of animals, to use them for food, work and clothing. In his use of plants, too, man took an important step by giving up his habit of living off nature and starting to work together with it.

All this helped to stem the traditional wanderings from place to place. The first well-populated villages were born with the first forms of craftsmanship and the first tribal organizations. Archaeologists have unearthed implements used by Neolithic men in the first forms of agriculture.

When the most beautiful porcelain was made

One of the most interesting chapters in archaeological discoveries deals with cups, bowls and pots. From the rough stone bowls of the Palaeolithic Age to the delicate Chinese porcelain, the history of ceramics vividly records man's progress and his gradual artistic refinement.

The civilization which far outshone any other in this art was without doubt the Chinese.

The perfection which these articles attained in the course of a thousand years did not substantially alter the original ingredients: kaolin and petuntse.

A great civilization grew up in the Indus valley with beautiful cities and its own writing. The most famous city is Mohenjo-Daro in the Sind (today West Pakistan) where the bath-house illustrated here is to be found.

Kaolin is a white clay and petuntse a feldspathic rock which takes on a glassy sheen when heated to 1,450 degrees C.

The period of greatest splendour of Chinese porcelain coincided with the famous Sung dynasty (A.D. 960–1279).

When the Egyptian civilization began

Largely due to the work of the archaeologists, we have been able to know one of the most splendid civilizations of all time. Priceless treasures of culture and art have been dug up from the Egyptian civilization which flourished on the banks of the Nile 3,000 years before Christ.

Perhaps no other ancient civilization has been so rich in the information it left behind it: from the temples to the tombs, from the jewels to the writing, all reflects a life of the greatest refinement.

Today we have a detailed picture of ancient Egypt, not just the important personages, the Pharaohs and priests, but also of the humbler people. This reconstruction has been made possible by the patience and skill of the archaeologists, particularly in the last two centuries. The tombs of the Pharaohs, with their friezes of the daily life, are a marvellous collection of pictures from which we can visualize how the ancient Egyptians lived.

Work and play, activity and repose, life and death speak to us clearly from the pictures which decorate the Egyptians' last resting places.

The picture language is a record of bustling activity in all walks of life, from the thousands of slaves condemned to build enormous pyramids, to the more powerful and refined who ruled like gods over a whole race.

The ideal life of the Egyptians, as recorded by the numerous written descriptions, the paintings and the objects which have come

Gold dagger of Tutankhamen (about 1350 B.C.), Cairo Museum

down to us through archaeology, was a simple existence. Pleasant and beautiful things were enjoyed but not to excess. The brick-built houses were owned by the state officials, the court dignataries, the merchants and the people in high places.

There were often charming oases where the master enjoyed the pleasures of family life. The slaves, the hunting and fishing, are all well documented by the inscriptions and paintings.

Funeral temple of Hatshepsut

When the temple of Hatshepsut was built

The great Pharaohs have always been famous in the history of Egypt. Man-gods, they were surrounded by great pomp and ceremony. But the history of ancient Egypt was also written by the mighty Queens, about whom the archaeological evidence is impressive and vivid.

One of the most important examples is certainly the temple built by order of Hatshepsut, the first woman destined to rule Egypt.

This sovereign of the eighteenth dynasty of the Pharaohs, reigned from about 1503 to 1482 B.C., shortly after her predecessors had succeeded in driving out the Hyksos, the Shepherd kings who had occupied Egypt.

Her funeral temple, rising at the feet of the towering cliffs near Thebes and built by the architect Senenmut, demonstrates how colossal and perfect the art of ancient Egypt was.

When the art of the goldsmith began in Europe

It is unfortunately a fact that, even in the most ancient temples, thieves and vandals have forced open countless tombs to steal objects of gold and other precious materials. In spite of this, archaeologists are still able to show us all kinds of jewellery as living proof of past civilizations.

The gold work of the Etruscans is famous. By 700 B.C. they had reached a standard of workmanship which was unequalled for centuries. A typical Etruscan jewel was the fibula, a brooch of which some splendid examples have been found, finely worked and richly encrusted with stones.

Etruscan earrings are some of the most interesting pieces of jewellery of all times. The beauty of these ornaments lies not only in the accuracy of the work but also in the variety of shapes.

More typical than any other ornament, however, was the *bulla*, a bulb-shaped pendant of leather or metal. If was regarded as a mascot which was probably designed to hold amulets or filled with a liquid, such as perfume.

When the goldsmith's art flourished in northern Europe

The people of northern Europe were very skilful at working in gold. Before the Romans had landed on their island, the ancient Britons had specialized in making rings, bracelets and 'torques', which were necklaces in the form of a twisted band, like collars.

A people may express its own culture and taste even through the simplest objects. This was the case of the Britons, who managed to make tiny masterpieces of gold from such an everyday object as a pin. What we know today as the safety-pin became ornaments of great beauty, much prized for fastening heavy cloaks.

A similar taste may be observed in all the Nordic peoples, although the shape of the pins varies from place to place, from the elongated, cross-shaped pins of the Britons to the flat, roundish pins of the Danes.

The most important collection of gold work in northern Europe was discovered in the ship burial of Sutton Hoo in Suffolk. This grave of an Anglo-Saxon king contained gold and silver weapons.

When the Vikings became goldsmiths

It seems almost impossible that adventurous explorers like the Vikings, should be able to concentrate on an art which requires patience, meticulous skill and accuracy.

Yet archaeology has given us extraordinary proof of what these people were able to do with gold.

The evolution of the pin, for example, finds its most refined expression in the Viking culture: the bear's-head pins, drum pins and tortoise pins are even today some of the most original ever made.

Probably the most unusual creations of the Scandinavian goldsmiths, however, are the bracteates, medallions or coins stamped only on one side and often gold or silver-plated.

The Scandinavian bracteates, dating back to about the year 1000 B.C. mostly illustrate scenes or figures from Scandinavian mythology, such as the God Thor riding a goat.

On nearly all the jewellery of northern Europe real or mythological animals are portrayed, either by casting or by engraving.

When the Mayan civilization developed

Of particular interest to the archaeologist is the vast area of central South America, where survive the magnificent remains of the civilizations which flourished before Columbus.

Despite the damage done to the ancient buildings by the fierce campaigns of the Spanish conquerors and the erosion of time, it is still possible to reconstruct the fascinating history of these ancient peoples. Unknown to us until the discovery of America in 1492, the Mayas, the Aztecs and the Incas reached a very high standard of civilization. They originated in early Christian times and were still flourishing at the time of the Spanish conquerors.

The Mayan culture has left us surprising evidence in paintings, architecture and sculpture. The religious and ritual ceremonies, for example, are pictured with great realism and startling effect.

The pyramid-shaped buildings are especially interesting. Consisting of a series of terraces on top of each other, they remind us of the Egyptian pyramids, although they are built quite differently.

When the Aztec civilization flourished

Another great civilization which flourished at the same time as the Mayan was the Aztec. Both of them were situated roughly where modern Mexico is now.

The impressive buildings which survive them are all that is left of a splendour which will never die. It seems impossible that such greatness should have been ruined by civilized Europeans. Ignorant and fanatical, the Spanish conquerors gave vent to their greed and, for the sake of plunder, broke up a priceless treasure.

The archaeological remains tell us that one of the most beautiful cities of all the pre-Columbian civilizations was Tenochtitlan, which means 'stone rising in the water'. It was founded by the Aztecs on an island in lake Texcoco. The magnificence of its buildings and the richness and splendour of their decorations made this the capital city of an empire.

Not only the temples were built of stone at Tenochtitlan, but also the houses. Coated with a dazzling whitewash, they were graceful and attractive. Their terraces and gardens were gay with flowers and each neighbourhood was served by a network of navigable canals. The private houses were the fabric of the whole city, the heart of which was an immense square resplendent with the large, gold-decorated temple.

When the Inca civilization was brought to light

The third great civilization of America before Columbus, that of the Incas, grew up in the area now covered by Peru and its surrounding territories. It is more difficult to date it, as the Incas had no system of writing and so archaeological excavations have been the only means of reconstructing their history.

The most reliable estimate of the start of the Inca civilization puts it at about A.D. 1200. The most important discoveries and the ones which have provided the most information were made by an American archaeologist, Professor Hiram Bingham, of the University of Yale.

In 1911 he was lucky enough to find the remains of an Inca city, Machu Picchu, which means

Ancient Peak'. It lies about 100 kilometres from Cuzco, ancient capital of the Inca empire at the height of its splendour. Perched on an almost inaccessible mountain top, it was the last hideout of the fleeing Incas during the Spanish occupation. For four centuries it remained unknown and forgotten, even by the Indians of the Andes, the Incas' descendants.

One of the unsolved mysteries is how the Incas managed to transport the enormous blocks with which their walls, houses and stairways were built. They were hewn from quarries about 600 metres lower down the mountain. How they managed to carry them up to the top with the kinds of transport available in those days is still unexplained.

Most of the Inca people were farmers but every man had to serve periodically in the army or on building or mining. They built not only cities but suspension bridges, irrigation canals and fortresses.

When the ancient temples of the East grew up

The archaeologist who examines a site used for religious ceremonies normally expects some extraordinary surprises. This is what happened, for example, to the scholars who explored the gorgeous temples of the East with their extravagant architecture.

The uninhibited symbolism revealed in the countless statues, spires, turrets and other architectural embellishments, is a hard test for the scholar who wants to find the collective and individual meaning of these unusual works of art.

It is an oriental characteristic to express emotions as dramatically as possible whether in paintings, sculptures or architecture. The sculptures of the fantastic animals which decorate the temples are world-famous for their grotesque, terrifying faces.

A magnificent but by no means

unique example, is the famous temple at Madurai in India. Built in the shape of a rectangle measuring 260 metres long by 230 wide and surrounded by an arcade supported by 1,000 columns, the gigantic temple soars up, thick with spires and turrets, like an inaccessible mountain. The nine pyramid-shaped towers are mirrored in an inner pool of clearest water. Here is a whole world waiting to be interpreted by the archaeologist.

Temple of Minaksi at Madurai. It belongs to the seventeenth century and guards a collection of priceless jewels.

When the city of Zimbabwe arose

An ancient African city which still puzzles and fascinates the archaeologists is Zimbabwe, in south-eastern Zimbabwe. The enormous stone walls dating back to between A.D. 1100 and 1500 suggest a civilization which was certainly African although mixed with outside influences.

Recent research into the question has disproved the ancient legend which claimed that Zimbabwe was the last trace of the fabulous kingdom of Ofir and the site of King Solomon's mines.

Its reputation had attracted the attention of a private society which, towards the end of the nineteenth century, had devastated Zimbabwe and the surrounding area in its search for gold and other treasures.

What remains of the ancient civilization is gathered together with the utmost care by the archaeologists. The most usual findings are gold ornaments and pieces of jewellery with engraved patterns. From their discoveries archeologists hope to learn the history of one of the most ancient and advanced peoples of Africa.

When the Moslem civilization began in the Sudan

Africa is an immense, almost untouched field of research which daily proves to be increasingly important for our understanding of unknown cultures and civilizations.

The Sudan is one of the few regions of Africa scientifically explored in the nineteenth century. The German explorer and archaeologist, Heinrich Barth, after years spent in the Sudan, brought back a book of detailed notes. In it he meticulously described the features of the area he had explored.

Nothing escaped his careful investigation: the houses, the villages, the tribal customs, are all listed, together with purely geographical notes about rivers, mountains, vegetation, distances and so on.

With the help of this work Europeans were able to learn about the Sudan at a time when Africa was for the most part still unknown. Around Timbuktu today there are still buildings which are of great interest from an archaeological point of view. Some of these are mosques which are a sign of an active trade with the Moslem Arabs.

Massive wall at Zimbabwe, dating back to A.D. 1500

When archaeology joined forces with atomic science

The atomic scientists who discovered nuclear energy may have been aware of its enormous potential, but they certainly could not have foreseen the infinite uses to which this energy would be put within the space of a few years. If they had been told that nuclear energy would even be used in archaeology, the inventors of the atomic bomb would have had serious doubts.

Yet today this is a tool which has provided definite proof. It all started with the discovery that living organisms contain Carbon 14, which is produced by the neutral particles in cosmic rays penetrating Earth from outer space.

Since Carbon 14 is reduced by half over a period of 5,568 years, archaeological discoveries can be dated by measuring how much Carbon 14 is still contained in them.

The oldest African mosque at Timbuktu to have lasted until the present day is built of sun-baked bricks

Skeleton surrounded by objects (above) Radio-carbon dating is now used to ascertain the age of skeletons and other archaeological discoveries (below)

The apparatus used in this delicate task has only been working for a few years but it has already given invaluable service to archaeology.

Establishing the age of the discoveries, which may date back 30,000 years, has often been essential for deeper and more accurate knowledge.

Although this highly delicate method still has some limitations, it is true to say that it has already introduced the archaeology of tomorrow.

Other recent technical inventions are also being used. The ground containing traces of ancient buried civilizations can be picked out from aerial photographs taken from great heights. Even the artificial satellites are proving to be extremely helpful in this field, with the information and photographs they are continually sending back to Earth.

Special camera equipment helps explore ancient tombs, underground passages and chambers which were the work of man. There is no longer any need for the traditional excavations which often risked permanent damage to the priceless buried treasures.

Even the computer has now been put to use by archaeology. Recently the whole of the Great Pyramid of Cheops was X-rayed centimetre by centimetre by a complex computer capable of revealing not only the composition of the blocks used to build it, but also whether unknown cavities were hidden inside the monument.

This is only one example. The future alone can tell how much computers have to contribute to the development of the science of archaeology.

Enormous strides have been made along the road leading to

the discovery of the ancient civilizations. Archaeology has revealed the existence of unknown peoples, their ways of life, their dress and even the reasons for their disappearance.

It would seem as if little is left to be told about the mysteries of the past, as if there could be no new civilizations to dig up. Yet the experts insist, with undeniable proof, that archaeology today is still in its infancy and that it has reached a turning-point in its methods of research.

Scientific discoveries and technical advance provide the students of the past with an impressive array of tools. But the archaeological conquests of tomorrow will be all the greater as an increasing number of specialists go to work in the field and find themselves having to work as a team.

The figure of the romantic archaeologist is becoming more and more a memory of the past.

WHEN WAR BEGAN

When did war begin? This is a question which has never been answered. It is probably as old as man and may be older.

According to some scholars,

Mars, God of War

the first war was fought towards the end of the Great Ice Age: two tribes of apes, one vegetarian and living in the forests, and one meat-eating and living on the plains, fought over a territory which was gradually shrinking as the sheets of ice advanced. Although this is pure guess-work, war has existed since the earliest signs of human civilization.

The majority of archaeological discoveries consists of weapons which were not necessarily used for hunting animals. The Bible, Egyptian, Babylonian and Hittite history, the Homeric poems are all full of descriptions of battles and wars, which have influenced the course of history. But, although war is a constant theme in the history of man, his ways of fighting it have altered profoundly. In the Stone Age it was customary for the winners to devour the losers at the end of a battle; today the Geneva Convention controls the treatment of prisoners of war, although it cannot be said that it is always strictly observed. In the Age of Chivalry battles were fought by a rigid code of rules, but today men can fight without even seeing their enemy.

War is therefore an interesting guide to the technological progress, dress and morals of the people fighting it and as such it is extremely important to students. But it is also the most tragic, horrifying and inconclusive act that man can ever commit.

When a handful of men changed the history of the world

Battles which have made their mark on the destiny of the world are rare in the history of man. One of these rare cases is the battle of Gaugamela.

It was the year 331 B.C. Alexander the Great had been sitting on the doorstep of the vast Persian Empire for several years past but now he had issued an historical challenge to his giant foe. The kingdom of the Persian Emperor, Darius III, was so vast that it had taken him many years to call together an army from all his people. But, at last, at the head of an army larger than any previously assembled, numbering more than half a million foot soldiers, 45,000 horsemen, 15 elephants and 200 war-chariots, he hurried to squash finally the annoying mosquito which had dared to bother him.

Against this huge army Alexander pitted a small formation, the spearhead of which was the Macedonian phalanx: 9,000 men armed with very long lances and arranged in eight columns along a one-kilometre front.

The morning of the battle dawned. In the weak October sun the Macedonians watched the huge Persian army launch itself into the attack with a tremendous roar. The wing of the Macedonian army broke under this human sea. Darius was certain of victory. But suddenly the phalanx appeared.

Behind the terrifying iron wall of their lances, the Macedonians aimed at the opposing army. Darius' lines wavered, then broke. It was all over! One of the greatest empires ever to have existed had miserably crumbled.

When proud Rome was brought to its knees

At the Caudine Forks the Romans underwent a humiliating experience. Ambushed by the Samnites in 321 B.C., they were compelled to pass, one by one, under a yoke formed by two crossed swords, as a sign of submission. They were then free to return home.

The only compensation the Samnites demanded was that the Romans should finally decide to lay down their arms for ever. In view of their sorry situation, the Consuls accepted and peace was signed, but the Roman senate, which had not had to go under the yoke, thought it better to reopen hostilities.

And so proud and haughty Rome, having suffered such a humiliating defeat, was further

· **Roman soldier**

disgraced by breaking its word. It was the two poor Consuls, Veturius and Postumius, who had to pay the price of this dishonourable about-face: they were sent back to the Samnites as a punishment for having agreed to lay down their arms.

When the trumpets of Rome put Hannibal to flight

The battle of Zama, in 202 B.C., was the decisive battle in the Second Punic War. It was an important moment for Roman history because it marked the final defeat of Carthaginian power.

It would be impossible to describe it in a few lines, but there was one strange event which played a big part in the outcome of that encounter.

The armies of Hannibal and Scipio were facing each other; the forces were slightly in favour of Carthage, which had 50,000 men against the 45,000 of Rome. Above all, it had one exceptional weapon: its elephants.

But those very elephants were the ruin of Carthage. The cunning Scipio knew what they were like and, when he saw them advancing, he gave orders to his trumpeters to blow their bugles with all their might.

The awful noise terrified the huge animals who fell back, trampling on the Carthaginian cavalry behind them.

Seeing their confusion and surprise, Scipio sent in his troops to the attack. The Carthaginians were defeated and their might was crushed for ever.

When Europe was saved from the Arabs

It was the year A.D. 732; the Arab Empire was at its peak. The Moorish armies, under the command of the Caliph Abder Rahaman, had occupied Spain, crossed the Pyrenees and descended into France. The road to the plains of Central Europe was wide-open to invasion. Against this threat was Charles Martel, grandfather of Charlemagne, at the head of a coalition of the peoples of France.

It was a clash between two different civilizations, different not only in their religions and cultures but also in the way they fought. On one side the Moors, lightly armed, placed their trust in their archers and horsemen, armed with javelins and scimitars. On the other side was the powerful apparatus of war of the tall, strong Franks, completely protected by steel, armed with broad shields and long, heavy swords or terrifying battle-axes; these warriors were mounted on powerful horses which were much taller than the highly-strung Arab ponies.

For several days the Moslems had been trying to provoke the Frankish warriors and make them come down from the hills of Poitiers, where they were drawn up in a long, unbroken wall of steel. They wanted to engage them in hand-to-hand combat, at which they were experts, but Charles Martel did not yield and, on the morning of 7 October, the little Arab horsemen finally took the initiative and launched themselves into the attack.

For hour after hour the Moors battled against the giants without managing to break their array. Then, towards sunset, the Franks suddenly stirred and attacked in serried ranks. The impact of the Christians was so great that the Moslems panicked. As darkness fell the hills of Poitiers were littered with the corpses of retreating Arabs and the Empire of the Crescent Moon saw its dream of a conquered Europe crumble.

Charles Martel had broken the Moslem invasion of France, saved Aquitaine, and established his title as defender of Christendom.

When Turkish rule in the Mediterranean was ended

More than 800 years had passed since the battle of Poitiers. The Turks had taken the place of the Arabs in controlling the southern Mediterranean but the old rivalries between Christian and Moslem were not dead yet. One of the greatest naval conflicts in history was about to take place: the battle of Lepanto on 7 October 1571.

The forces in the field were more or less equal: estimates vary slightly, but there were about 240 Christian galleys plus 6 larger galleasses to about 260 Moslem ships. The battle was fierce and lasted many hours. The Christians were suddenly put at an advantage, however, by the arrival of the

Sixteenth-century Venetian galley

of the Turkish galleys were rows of slaves, mostly Christian prisoners who certainly did not look favourably on their masters. The oarsmen in the Christian ships, on the other hand, were mainly volunteers or prisoners who knew they would regain their freedom if the Christian squadron won.

This situation was to the Europeans' advantage for two reasons. Firstly, in the hand-to-hand fighting, they could rely on the help of the oarsmen, who were allowed

galleasses which, unlike the galleys, bristled with cannons both on their prows and on their broadsides.

This initial superiority was then strengthened still more by another advantage. In those days, although the ships had sails, they were propelled mainly by oars. Altogether there were more oarsmen than soldiers on the ships at Lepanto. But between the two armies there was one great difference: chained to the benches

to be armed. Secondly, the Christians at the oars of the Turkish ships sometimes managed to free themselves, settling skirmishes which were vital to the Europeans. These two factors, combined with the great courage of the fighters, helped Don John of Austria, commander of the Spanish, Venetian, Papal, Genoese, Maltese and Florentine allies, to get the better of the valiant Ali Pasha and finally to break Moslem power in the Mediterranean.

When Canada became a British colony

During the Seven Years War, (1756–63), the Prussians' English allies attacked the French in their overseas possessions. Of these, one of the most important was Canada, with its beautiful city of Quebec on the St. Lawrence river. At Quebec the French had a well-seasoned garrison under the command of General Montcalm. England, however, had already set her sights on Canada.

At the end of the summer of 1759, a British naval squadron sailed up the St. Lawrence, heading towards the city. A strong contingent of troops landed under the command of General Wolfe, who surrounded the city and attempted to attack it from the front. The manoeuvre was unsuccessful and, in the course of a fierce battle, the English were driven back.

So Wolfe made his troops set sail again and head back down the St. Lawrence. The French general, Montcalm, detailed a large number of men to follow the British retreat and General Wolfe seized his opportunity.

He sailed secretly back up the river, landed a little more than a mile from Quebec and climbed the heights of Abraham to the plains above. The French came out of the city to give battle and throughout 13 September the two armies fought bravely until the British troops eventually gained the upper hand. On 17 September the French evacuated and the next day the city surrendered.

At the end of the conflict among the dead were the two generals, Wolfe and Montcalm.

This battle was of great historical importance for the Americans. Following it, in 1760, Amherst captured Montreal for the British. France had to give up her claim to Canada, which became a British colony, and French colonial power declined in America.

When a handful of Swedes routed the Russian Army

It happened at Narva, a little town on the icy Gulf of Finland, in the winter of 1700.

The town's small garrison, a thousand of the Swedes' allies, was besieged by an army of 60,000 Russians under General Dolgorovky. The Russians wanted to snatch the base from the Swedish King Charles XII. The story is one of the most glorious pages in Swedish and world history.

The winter was particularly severe that year. The snow had fallen very thickly and made the roads impassable. Nevertheless, Charles XII, aware of the danger threatening his allies at Narva, did not hesitate to march to their aid.

Hindered by the cold, the mud and the snow, the expedition came in sight of Narva on 20 November. Without a moment's rest and deliberately ignoring the superior numbers of its opponents, it moved in to attack the Russians who were besieging the town.

Against the 60,000 soldiers and 145 cannons of the Czar, Charles XII had only thirty-seven cannons and 10,000 men: six Russians for every Swede!

The relief force threw itself into the attack. The besieging Russians, surprised by the vigour and bravery of their enemy, fled in disorder after three hours' hard fighting.

The collapse of a bridge on the road of retreat hampered the Russians' flight and many of the fleeing soldiers died a miserable death in the frozen waters.

Narva and its heroic defenders were saved, while the Russians paid for the bravery of the Swedish soldiers with 18,000 dead. The

Eighteenth-century Swedish grenadier

Swedes, on their part, had only lost 2,000.

This victory gave the Swedes supremacy in the Baltic.

When the power of the United States began

Saratoga, 1777. The American War of Independence was smouldering. The Redcoats, the universal symbol of the mighty British Empire, were completely out of their depth. They were faced not by any regular army but by a collection of colonials determined to defend their rights and ready to drive the English off their land at all costs.

Up until then, however, all that had happened was petty harassing or guerilla attacks. The English were convinced that, once they had forced their opponents out into the open, their superior knowledge of military tactics would triumph.

But they were wrong. They sailed off down the Hudson but were defeated by the rebels for the first time on 19 September in the battle of Freeman's Farm, and again on 7 October at Bemis Heights. Then they were forced to retire to Saratoga.

Nor were they allowed to rest there. The rebels, led by General Gates, laid siege to the town and, after some violent skirmishes, succeeded in breaking the enemy resistance. General Burgoyne had no alternative but to surrender and hope that the Americans would let him withdraw with his troops.

Gates did not hesitate. He knew that the English were men of honour and, as soon as he had their promise that they would never again take up arms against the colonies, he allowed them to return home.

So American power began. It was a power born of a generous, human gesture which did credit both to the victors and the vanquished.

Austrian Dragoons officer (1805)

When the wind joined forces with Napoleon

In the days of the great sailing ships, the direction of the wind or a change in the weather were deciding factors in the outcome of battles. Not everyone knows, however, that the wind played an important part at Marengo, too, where Napoleon inflicted a heavy defeat on the Austrian army.

Resting in Italy after the Egyptian campaign, Napoleon found himself confronted by a strong Austrian army entrenched in Alessandria.

This time the great general disobeyed his own rules. Once in sight of the city, he set up camp near the village of Marengo and dispatched General Desaix with a strong contingent to check that the Austrians were not leaving. His own forces were thus split.

So on the morning of 14 June 1800, when General Melas marched out of Alessandria at the head of 30,000 Austrians, Napoleon had only 19,000 men with whom to oppose him. He quickly sent messengers to Desaix, but he knew they had little chance of reaching him in time.

The battle began at eight o'clock in the morning. By five in the evening all seemed lost for Napoleon. Melas returned to Alessandria to announce his victory. But suddenly, in a cloud of dust, Desaix appeared, after a forced march to help the French. The tables were turned and the Austrians surrendered under the onslaught of the fresh reinforcements.

The French lost about 4,000 men, including Desaix who fell in the attack; the Austrians lost 9,500.

Napoleon won with the help of the wind. Desaix, in fact, had not received the messages but had heard the noise of the shooting carried across to him by the wind, which was fortunately blowing in the right direction!

Soldiers of the nineteenth-century French army

When Nelson fought his last battle

Trafalgar is one of the best known battles in history. It took place off Cape Trafalgar, south of Cadiz, on 21 October 1805, when the English dealt a mortal blow to the might of Napoleon. It was on this occasion that Nelson sent the famous signal to his fleet: 'England expects that every man will do his duty.'

In the middle of the fierce fighting the French vessel *Redoutable* became locked in battle with the *Victory*, Nelson's flag-ship. After a bloody clash the French were driven back, but a shot from a sniper's musket in the *Redoutable's* topmast had mortally wounded Nelson.

If at this point the flag of the British admiral had been lowered, there was a risk that the other British ships would have given up the fight at the crucial moment. So the news of Nelson's fatal wound was withheld from the English fleet.

It was only at the end of the battle that the victorious English learned of the death of their admiral, Napoleon's enemy till the bitter end.

When Napoleon lost his Empire

The Battle of Waterloo, which brought an end to the Napoleonic Empire, is famous in history for the savage violence of the fighting, which involved hundreds of thousands of men and lasted on and off for three days, from 15 to 18 June 1815.

Napoleon's army was 120,000 men and 570 cannon strong, while the Anglo-Prussian allies had a total of 220,000 men and 500 cannons.

Until sunset on the third day, on the field of La Haye Sainte, Bonaparte had managed to save his empire.

For more than twelve hours, without food or drink, the soldiers of both sides had been slaughtering each other. Yet the initial

The *Ohio* (above, left); French battleship (above, right); the *Victory* (below)

positions remained unchanged, apart from the piles of dead and wounded mixed with the acrid smoke of the cannon fire and the dust churned up by the cavalry charges.

At seven in the evening, after trying all day, the French broke through. Although pressed in the rear by the Prussians, Napoleon's victory was in his grasp. All that remained was to send in the Old Guard, the pride of his army.

But, for the first and last time in his life, the Emperor hesitated. After nearly an hour, when he ordered the attack, it was already too late. The English troops under Wellington had been reinforced with the help of the Prussians, and the French charge was repelled. The evening of 18 June 1815 saw the massacre of the Imperial Guard and the crumbling of a world. One hour of indecision had changed the course of history.

When the military might of Germany was born

Germany was born one rainy day in July 1866. Prussia and the Austro-Hungarian Empire were fighting for control of the German principalities. After occupying the territories which now make up Western Germany, the Prussian army turned south, divided into three columns. Waiting for it was a strong Austrian army.

The Prussians won and they won because of their own mistake. In command of the Prussian army was Count von Moltke, an experienced, careful strategist who had a very definite plan: to keep the three columns of his army separate on the march and then reunite them for the battle. But Prince Karl, at the head of one of these columns, thought otherwise.

As soon as he was within reach of the enemy he joined up with the nearest column and moved into the attack in a position of weakness.

Defeat seemed certain but Moltke knew how to make the most of even a calamity like that. He ordered the column which had stayed in the rear to advance quickly.

While Prince Karl engaged the main body of the Austrian army, he waited hopefully. Towards evening, when the situation seemed desperate, the reinforcements arrived and the Austrians were defeated.

So a tactical error turned into one of the most brilliant military masterstrokes and marked the start of German power.

Soldiers of the 92nd Highlanders

When the cholera killed more than the guns

Fact and fiction merge in the famous story of the 'Charge of the Six Hundred'. In fact, the charge of the British Light Brigade at Balaclava on 25 October 1854 was only a minor event in the Crimean War: a useless massacre caused by a mistaken order.

The Russians had just been driven back near Balaclava by a regiment of Scottish Fusiliers. Some guns which had fallen into Czarist hands still had to be recovered, however. The order was misunderstood and Lord Cardigan, in command of a cavalry unit, thought he was being told to charge a strong Russian position. Without questioning the absurd order or the suicidal mission on which he was being sent, the English commander arranged his men in order of combat. The charge rightly became a legend.

The Crimean War (1854–6)

The 600 British cavalrymen galloped towards the Russian cannons; after crossing a narrow valley under the cross-fire of the artillery, they reached the position, leaving nearly half of their comrades dead on the field.

The incident left an impression of stupidity as well as courage, so that General Pierre Bosquet said of it, *'C'est magnifique mais ce n'est pas la guerre.'*

But glorious and legendary though it was, it was only a brief incident in the Crimean War. The Turks, the French, the British and, later on, the Piedmontese, were all fighting against the Russians who had occupied the Peninsula.

The war lasted two years, 1854–6, and brought with it a change in the methods of warfare. In fact, besides the incidents like the glorious charge of Balaclava, which recalled the glories of a now distant Napoleonic past, there were the first signs of the war of the trenches which became famous in 1914–18.

For the first time the soldiers of five countries were tasting the horrors of a trench thick with mud or a dug-out bombarded by shelling. But far more terrible was another danger which harassed the armies: the cholera.

The Crimean War was the first to be recorded by the camera. The pictures we have are of soldiers and officers resting, with neat uniforms, polished rifles and proud faces. The reality of the war was very different, however: horrifying massacres made possible by greater artillery power, military hospitals full of untended wounded and, worst of all, endless rows of dead, killed not by the guns but by the cholera which was, ultimately, the only true victor of that wretched war.

When the International Red Cross was founded

If the Battle of Balaclava reminds us of the glorious, romantic gestures of the past, the Battle of Solferino shows the reality of a war which mercilessly crushed men and hopes.

On the west bank of the Mincio, on the morning of 24 June 1859, were gathered the French Emperor, Napoleon III, the King of Sardinia, Victor Emmanuel II, and the Austrian Emperor, Franz Josef.

The Franco-Piedmontese army and the Austrian army were equal in strength and were marching against each other, bent on destruction. It was a ruthless, head-on clash: after an initial period of isolated but nonetheless cruel skirmishes, the positions became more clearly defined.

The Austrians were being forced to split their forces to face the Italians at San Martino and the French at Solferino, and they were steadily losing ground. The French artillery was shattering the Austrian infantry.

Under the onslaughts of the French troops the Austrians were forced to retreat from their original positions. Finally, towards midday, Napoleon launched his men against the centre of the Austrian army, after an intense barrage of artillery fire. The battle raged fiercely but, in the end, hard-pressed by the dashing Algerian Zouaves, Franz Josef was forced to order the retreat to the other side of the Mincio.

More than 40,000 men lay dead or wounded. So much blood had been spilt that Napoleon hastened to offer an armistice which the Austrians accepted.

Men began to be afraid of war and the Swiss banker, Jean Henri Dunant, who witnessed the sufferings at Solferino, was so moved by the massacre that he began to outline the principles which were to become the foundation of the International Red Cross.

When war moved from the ground to the sky

The Franco-Prussian war of 1870–71 is famous not only for the long siege of Paris but also for the appearance of a new, unusual instrument of war: the balloon. Previously captive balloons, fastened to the ground by long cables, had been used for observation, but now they took on strategic importance.

To defend the capital there were 550,000 Frenchmen against some 240,000 assailants. The situation was serious because communications with the rest of France were practically impossible.

General Ducrot's attempt to relieve German pressure on the capital by engaging the enemy in a great offensive to the east, failed at Villiers when 10,000 Frenchmen and 6,000 Germans died.

A harsh defeat seemed to be in store for France, but there was still a chance that the blockade of Paris could be raised by calling up reinforcements from all over the country. To mobilize the relief, there had to be some means of communication which could cross the enemy lines. And so the balloons appeared.

The first took off on 23 September 1870. It flew over the Prussian lines and landed 8 kilometres away on French soil. Throughout the siege the French used balloons to maintain a link between the besieged city and the provinces. Sixty-six were used in four months and only six of them fell into German hands. More than a hundred people managed to leave Paris in this way. In addition, 2,500,000 letters reached the provinces, together with many carrier pigeons who then brought messages back to the capital.

When an athletics society challenged the great powers

Towards the end of the last century China was rapidly beginning to feel the influence of European nations.

European penetration had already occurred in the south: the French, having occupied Indochina, now controlled vast areas of southern China. In the eastern part of the country, several European countries had moved from the coastal towns and had penetrated the interior.

This situation greatly worried the crumbling Chinese empire, whose rulers planned to stir up a revolt against the whites. It was not difficult to find the men for the job.

At that time in China there existed the Boxers, a secret society known in Chinese as the 'Fists of justice and order', which had begun as an athletics society but had quickly become a political organization.

The Boxers became the focal point of a big anti-foreigner movement, and in 1900 there broke out the famous rising which bears their name. It ravaged the Europeans living in China with death and terror.

When the rebels put the European legations in Peking under siege, the great powers decided to intervene, with the intention of turning the situation to their advantage.

An international military expedition was hurriedly got together: it seized the Chinese capital, forced the Court to flee and abandon the Boxers, to punish the leaders of the revolt, pay a very heavy indemnity, and make new and very major concessions to the Europeans.

When the first major clash between battleships occurred

The Russo-Japanese war (1904–5), in which Japan took its place as a major world power, saw the first known battleship clash of any magnitude.

A powerful fleet had left the Baltic Sea to go to the aid of the Russian troops and, after many adventures, it finally reached the China Sea, *en route* for Vladivostock. But the Japanese admiral, Togo, hidden with his fleet behind Tsushima Island, was expecting the enemy.

The opponents were about equal in strength but the Russians were worn out after their long voyage while Togo's men were fresh and fighting-fit.

The two squadrons met on the morning of 27 May 1905 but quite soon a thick blanket of fog had come down between them. The Russian admiral, Rozhestvenski, quickly started to change his formation but the move did not succeed. The fog lifted and the Japanese opened fire on the Russian ships in mid-manoeuvre.

The battle raged without stopping for two days and a night. In the end the superior speed and accuracy of the Japanese gunners won the day. The Russian admiral, wounded and unconscious, had to abandon three ships destroyed by enemy fire.

By the evening of 28 May, Russian sea-power was no more than a memory. Two-thirds of their fleet had been sunk, six ships had been captured, while six took refuge in neutral ports and only four reached Vladivostok. Japanese losses were slight but the Russians had 4,830 dead.

When the Verdun massacre was committed

The bloodshed and tragedy of the First World War are only too well-known, but there is one episode which, more than any other, reflects the horror and futility of slaughter in battle.

The most terrible massacre happened at Verdun and lasted non-stop for four months, from 21 February to 1 July 1916. Throughout this period forty-three German divisions tried to occupy the fortified square of Verdun, defended by seventy-three French divisions in furious bayonet attacks.

On both sides tens of thousands of shells swept the ground and razed mountains, pouring thousands of tons of fire and steel on the fighters.

The main focus of the battle was the Fort of Douaumont and the rise of Mort-Homme, which were gained, lost and regained time after time by the two sides.

All told, it was a useless massacre. On 1 July, when the Germans ended the offensive, the French lines had retreated only a few kilometres away from their original positions and, within months, the Allies had almost effortlessly regained the ground lost.

The only result of the Verdun massacre was the realization that war was no longer an exciting game but a futile and inhuman waste of lives.

At Verdun many lives were lost: the Germans left 278,000 dead and wounded on the field, the French 442,000: a human sacrifice equal to the population of a large city, a terrible warning against the atrocities of war.

French infantry soldier, 1917

When the greatest naval battle of the First World War was fought

As Verdun was a conflict between enormous masses of men, so the Battle of Jutland was a clash between the two most powerful fleets in the First World War.

It was the Germans who sought battle first. As Admiral Scheer left the harbours of the Baltic Sea, a powerful fleet under the command of Admiral Jellicoe headed out from the English coast. It was 31 May 1916. The forces in the field were equal; the Germans were at a slight disadvantage numerically but this was offset by the fact that the English were forced to wait for their opponents to make the first move.

In the first encounter the German Admiral Hipper succeeded in drawing the English squadron, commanded by Beatty, towards the body of the German fleet, when Scheer suddenly appeared on the horizon.

Beatty drew back towards Jellicoe's ships. The battle became general and more than 250 ships took part. At midnight the Germans retired, leaving the English masters of the field.

The British fleet had taken some hard knocks and its losses were far greater than those of its opponents. The two sides argued at length over who had won: the British declared they had because they had remained master of the field, the Germans claimed victory as they had fewer losses. The truth was, as usual, that the only one to win the fight was Death, who claimed nearly 9,000 casualties. The Battle of Jutland was as inconclusive in the war as the useless massacre of Verdun.

When the laws of chivalry governed aerial combat

The First World War was the test bench of many new weapons and new fighting techniques. During it a great new instrument of war appeared: the aeroplane.

The first fragile wooden aeroplane had passed a few war trials with the Italians in the Libyan campaign of 1911, but it was not until 1914 and after that this weapon was widely adopted for fighting the enemy on a new front. The rival nations concentrated on building more and more powerful and faster and faster aeroplanes, which battled with each other in the sky with their elementary weapons.

Innumerable acts of heroism were performed by the first airmen, who duelled with each other in fair fights, almost as in the olden days of chivalry. Each nation had its aces and its heroes: Italy had Francesco Baracca, England had Edward Mannock and the United States had Edward Rickenbaker. But the most famous of all was the German ace, von Richthofen, best known as the Red Baron, who nearly always fought in a Fokker. In three years of aerial combat he had eighty victories then he, too, was shot by an ordinary soldier on 21 April 1918.

After four years of war the aircraft industry had made amazing progress. 250 different kinds of aeroplane were on the drawing board and 160,000 built. And this was only the start: the next wars were to show how indispensable this new military force was to become.

Sopwith Pup

The battleship H.M.S. *Dreadnought*, completed in 1906

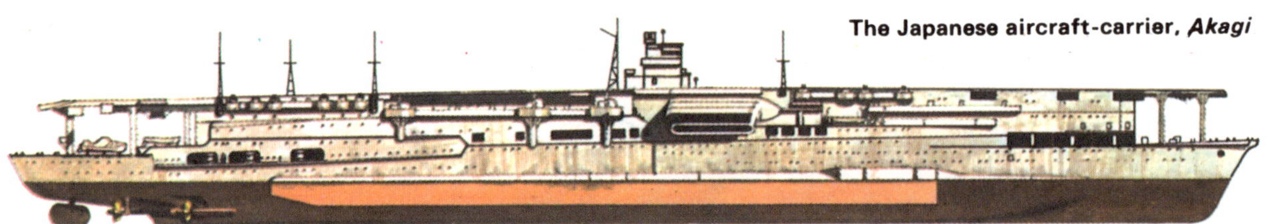

The Japanese aircraft-carrier, *Akagi*

When the aircraft-carriers decided the outcome of the war in the Pacific

Midway Atoll, in the middle of the central Pacific, is about 10 kilometres in diameter. It encloses two islands, Eastern and Sand, and is only a miserable, unimportant strip of land. Yet the battle fought over it between the 3 and 6 June 1942 was crucial for the outcome of the war in the Pacific.

Determined to wipe out the American fleet, the Japanese were moving towards Midway with a powerful array of aircraft-carriers, destroyers, cruisers and other impressive means of attack. Although weaker in numbers, the Americans had one advantage: they had broken the Japanese code and therefore knew their enemy's plans.

Not a single gunshot was exchanged between the two fleets.

The battle was fought at a distance by the aeroplanes on the carriers. The Americans managed to reach the enemy before the Japanese planes had succeeded in taking off, and so they won.

On the bridges of the ships all hell broke loose: bombs, fuel, torpedoes, planes, all exploded in a furnace of smoke and fire.

By evening four Japanese carriers and a cruiser had sunk. The Americans had lost their carrier *Yorktown* and an escorting destroyer.

The Japanese Admiral Nagumo tried to attack with his guns but his forces were too scattered. All he could do was call the retreat.

The Japanese had lost not only much of their carrier strength but also many of their best-trained naval pilots.

The Americans found themselves in command of the sea and from then on they were able to start recovering the ground lost in the area of the Pacific. The aircraft-carriers had proved how vitally important they were.

When the Allies landed in Normandy

1944 opened with Europe still controlled by the German troops. The Allied forces had landed in Sicily and were slowly marching up the Italian Peninsula. The Russians had broken the Nazi offensive towards the east but the key to the German continental system, France, was still firmly in the hands of Hitler. After much discussion, the Allies decided to land in Normandy.

The invasion was planned on a scale befitting the coastal fortifications prepared by the Germans in the famous Atlantic Wall. It eventually went according to plan but at the outset the margin between victory and defeat was dangerously narrow.

The operation, codenamed 'Overlord', began on the night of 5 and 6 June 1944—the famous D-Day of the Second World War— with an airdrop of parachutists and gliders behind the enemy lines. The actual landing started at daybreak. 700 warships and 4,066 landing craft took part in it, protected by an enormous airforce.

By the evening of the first day more than 150,000 men with tanks and artillery had landed, despite desperate enemy resistance. It was only after heavy fighting, however, that General Rommel ordered the retreat of the German troops: the liberation of Europe had begun.

When the bombers beat the fighters

In the long duel between offensive and defensive weapons, the battle between bombers and fighters deserves special mention, as it is still as tragic and topical as ever.

In theory the aeroplane defending its own territory starts off at a considerably advantage, from the aviation point of view alone. It does not have to carry a heavy supply of fuel on board, its load of ammunition can be kept to the minimum required for destroying the enemy planes, and the crew can be reduced to one man.

The bomber, on the other hand, needs fuel for a long flight, several crew members to cope with all the emergencies, and a load of bombs and machine guns on all sides because it is the fighter which chooses the point of attack. Yet, in spite of all these handicaps, there was a plane which managed to fly higher than nearly all the enemy fighters and nearly as fast as they did.

It was the Boeing B-29 Super-fortress, built by the Americans. It made its maiden flight in September 1942 and two years later went into action against the Japanese, causing tremendous destruction. It was from an aircraft of this type, the *Enola Gay*, that the atom bomb was dropped on Hiroshima on 6 August 1945.

Once again man had provided terrible proof of his inventiveness.

WHEN EXPLORING BEGAN

Primitive man's daily worry was how to survive physically. Feeding himself, bringing children into the world and providing for them, took up his whole attention for a long time. But every time man worried about his surroundings, he was unconsciously starting to discover the Earth.

What lay beyond the ring of mountains encircling the fertile valley? Where did the river run, from which he drank every day? What secrets were hidden in the vast sea which lapped the shore? What had the countless stars moving across the sky to do with the life of man? Would be Sun which rose in the morning come back and shine again after it had sunk below the horizon in the evening, leaving the Earth in darkness? Would the Moon dare to come out at night to comfort all the living creatures?

As primitive man tried to find the answer to these questions, he was exploring the Earth and making the first geographical discoveries.

The first people whose dress and way of life are well-known to us were comfortably settled on the land, from which they obtained food and prosperity. The farming peoples were often dissatisfied with their surroundings, however, and invented unknown worlds and lands full of riches.

Their stories magnified their desires, coloured them with magic and carried them off to wonderful adventures. That is how the most beautiful legends began. Although interwoven with fantasy, they all contain elements of truth.

The Golden Fleece which, according to legend, the Greek, Jason, travelled to find as far afield as the edge of the Black Sea, is probably a fable grown up round a simple labourers' implement. It was most likely the sheepskin, which gold prospectors used for sieving gold dust out of river sand.

One of the greatest stories of adventure and exploration is of Odysseus' wanderings. After the Trojan War, he visited many strange places and encountered innumerable obstacles before returning home to Ithaca.

When the first explorations were made

The first news of geographical discoveries of any importance dates back to about 600 B.C. It comes from Egypt, where during the reign of the Pharaoh, Necho II, an expedition was organized to sail round Africa, from the Red Sea to the Nile delta.

The Pharaoh entrusted the venture to the Phoenicians. He knew what good seamen they were and was perhaps afraid that the Egyptian boats, built to sail the waters of the Nile, might not stand up to the sudden storms of the ocean. The voyage ended happily but lasted three long years.

Necho not only realized how important it was to complete the voyage round Africa, but also started planning a very forward-looking canal which was to join the Nile to the Red Sea. It was only the terrible wars he had to wage against his country's enemies which prevented him from carrying out his project.

The Egyptians were the people with great ideas but it was the Phoenicians who performed the fantastic feats. They were a people who had settled on a coastal strip of land at the eastern end of the Mediterranean and who had many colonies, the most important being Tyre and Sidon.

In the sixth century B.C. they were already making regular journeys from the coast of Africa to Great Britain, especially to Devon and Cornwall which they called the 'Tin Islands'.

To do this they had constantly to pass the terrible Pillars of Hercules, which stand on opposite sides of the Strait of Gibraltar and were supposed to mark the end of the world.

Primitive Egyptian galley with papyrus sail used on the Nile in 3000 B.C. for carrying grain

Phoenician merchantman

When it was realized that the Earth is round

The ancients were so convinced that the Earth was flat that even in the third century B.C. anyone daring to suggest otherwise would have been thought crazy. Yet many sailors had no doubt about it. There was so much to support their belief that the Earth was round and not flat, as they had always been told.

What made them so sure?

Mainly the common observation that a sailing ship approaching shore shows its sails above the horizon first and then its hull. Similarly, when it leaves port, it looks to the sailors as if the Earth is slowly sinking into the sea.

Some of them also noticed that in travelling north or south new groups of stars came into sight over the horizon and they therefore concluded that the Earth's surface could not be flat but must be curved.

Then, too, was the fact that at one and the same moment the Sun beats straight down in some places while in others it appears to be lower on the horizon.

Also they knew that all the stars and planets are round. But some beliefs are often so deep-rooted that they override the obvious truth.

When the first maps were drawn

An important step in describing our geographical surroundings was made by the Greeks. They did not leave a stone unturned in their efforts to explain some of the basic problems of the world about them.

The first true geographical surveys were therefore made in Greece, the cradle of Western civilization. One of the first geographical maps, which has fortunately survived to the present day, shows a rough but nevertheless fairly accurate sketch of the Mediterranean basin. Beyond the Pillars of Hercules the River Ocean grips the land like a vice: no one had brought back any definite information on the geographical shape of those vast areas, so there were naturally some big mistakes which later discoveries have rectified.

The shape of the Mediterranean is much more accurate, however. Its main features, such as islands, peninsulas, gulfs and river mouths, are all located more or less in their correct places. There are some interesting attempts to trace the course of some of the main waterways: the Danube, the Nile and the rivers of Mesopotamia.

When Eratosthenes measured the circumference of the Earth

Alexander the Great of Macedonia certainly could not have imagined that a scientist among his followers would manage to calculate the distance round the Earth, using the knowledge he had acquired on so many voyages.

But this is what happened in about 240 B.C. when Eratosthenes found himself in Alexandria, Egypt, the city which the great leader had founded and named after himself. Eratosthenes settled there as librarian of the museum where he wrote on astronomy, mathematics, geography and other subjects.

With amazing brilliance, even by today's standards, Eratosthenes calculated that the distance round the Earth, or its circumference, must be about 250,000 Greek

stadia, equivalent to about 46,250 modern kilometres.

We now know that its circumference measures 40,075 kilometres. Considering the size of the measurements involved, Eratosthenes' mistake is so small that it does not matter.

How did he reach such an accurate answer despite the fact that his instruments of observation were poor? He had some definite facts from which to work. One of these was the distance between Alexandria and Syene, the modern Aswan (5,000 stadia, about 800 kilometres) and another was the knowledge that on 21 June, Midsummer's Day, when the Sun reaches the top of its curve (about midday), it shines into the bottom of the wells of Syene; in other words, the Sun's rays shine straight down on Earth. On the same day and at the same time he calculated the angle made with the horizon by the shadows cast by the Sun in Alexandria. He discovered that the angle was seven and a half degrees and concluded that the distance between Alexandria and Syene must be seven and a half degrees in terms of the distance round the Earth.

Put like this it seems easy but only a genius could have had such a brilliant idea.

When Africa was first explored

Ever since the earliest times Africa has been a land of promise. It was therefore only natural that the peoples living around the Mediterranean should feel a burning desire to explore it. The voyage round Africa in the sixth century before Christ was not an isolated incident: Other important expeditions preceded and followed it.

The Egyptians, for example, in the reign of the first lady Pharaoh, Hatshepsut (from about 1503 to 1481 B.C.), pushed inland to explore Nubia and the remote areas of Somalia, called the 'land of Punt', the 'land of aromatics and incense' mentioned in ancient Egyptian writings. There they were

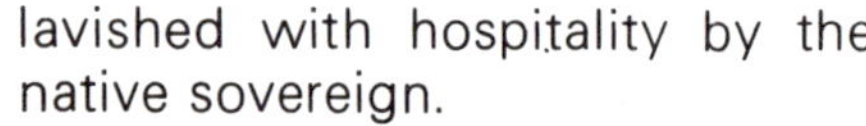

The Vikings reached America in the tenth century A.D. and must have met the red-skins (left)

lavished with hospitality by the native sovereign.

The main reason for this expedition was a search for precious wood which was known to be plentiful in those lands. The Egyptians must have been amazed to see the lake-dwellings of Punt built on stilts with the same wood that was so valuable to them.

Several centuries later, towards A.D. 150, the Greeks followed the coast of East Africa as far as Zanzibar.

The remains of numerous buildings are proof of the interest which Rome was bound to have taken in the African markets. Concrete evidence of how much was already known about Africa at the turn of the second century A.D. is the map which the great Ptolemy drew, using the wide geographical knowledge of the time.

When the Vikings reached North America

One group of people above all others has the distinction of having discovered an amazing number of new countries: it was the Vikings, with their natural thirst for adventure.

Even today it is not known quite how far they went with their daring expeditions. We know for certain, however, that around A.D. 1,000 they even touched the land which Christopher Columbus only reached 500 years later.

Born sailors, expert navigators, eager for adventure, they had already frequently visited the Mediterranean. They then set themselves to explore the unfriendly regions of the North.

One island which had a special fascination for them was Greenland. The first to reach it was Eric the Red, towards 980.

After a while, as nothing more was heard of him, Bjarni Herjolfsson set forth in search of the vanished sailor. By chance a storm tossed the Viking ships against an unknown coast, that of North America, but Bjarni did not want to land there.

The first European really to set foot on the country now called America was Eric the Red's second son, Leif Ericsson, although he did not realize the importance of this event.

With thirty-five men he had set out from Greenland, passing by Baffin Island, which he called 'the land of the flat stone'.

He then followed the coasts of Labrador and Newfoundland and spent much of the winter in what he named 'Vinland', or 'Wineland', because of the grapes which grew there. Scholars have situated Vinland on the coast of the present North America.

When Henry the Navigator took the first steps towards colonialism

At the time when sea trade was dominated by the maritime republics of Genoa and Venice, and North African trade was monopolized by the Arab merchants, Henry the Navigator (1394—1460) came on the scene.

Son of John I of Portugal, he

felt a burning desire for adventure. When he was only twenty-one years old he conquered Ceuta, the fortified North African port opposite Gibraltar, which had been an Arab possession for centuries. This thorn in the side of Europe had been an important factor in Arab expansion in Spain and Portugal.

For Henry, this early conquest was only the start of a scheme which filled his thoughts. He was sure that, beyond the immense Sahara, lived rich and prosperous nations with really fabulous gold mines.

Having seen the failures of other explorers, however, he moved cautiously. He encouraged marine engineering, founded a naval academy at Sagres and planned long sea voyages with the eye for detail of someone who knows he is embarking upon tremendous adventures.

Henry, who was called 'the Navigator' because of his passion for the sea, may rightly be regarded as the first conqueror and explorer of modern times.

When the Portuguese rounded Cape Verde

Such whole-hearted enthusiasm and complete dedication as those of Henry the Navigator could not fail to bring amazing results. The Portuguese sailors, although terrified by ancient superstitions and beliefs, ended up by actually wanting to go on the most daring adventures and the most dangerous voyages.

Spurred on by their passion for the sea, they discovered Madeira in 1420 and explored the Azores in 1427.

In 1434 a Portuguese ship commanded by Gil Eanes rounded Cape Bojador, opposite the Canary Islands. But the greatest victory against the ancient nightmares which preyed on the minds of the European sailors was the expedition of Dinis Dias: in 1445 he rounded Cape Verde, the most westerly point of Africa.

Dinis' voyage, which finally opened the doors of the immense riches of darkest Africa to the Europeans, was hailed by Henry the Navigator as the climax of his long, impassioned work. The way was clear and the superstitions defeated at last: the most wonderful opportunities now seemed possible.

The sea charts became more and more accurate and the navigational aids increasingly helpful until, in 1446, Alvaro Fernandes was able to probe his way along the coast of Africa nearly as far as the modern Sierra Leone.

This was the furthest point reached by Portuguese exploration in Prince Henry's lifetime.

When the caravel sailed

The maritime explorations promoted by Henry the Navigator would, by themselves, have been enough to ensure him a place in history. But he had another great distinction: he helped build a new type of ship, the caravel. Developed by the Portuguese for exploring the coast of Africa, the caravel was capable of standing up to long sea voyages and of achieving remarkable speed.

Henry probably guessed that the Atlantic would soon become the scene of the most glorious sea adventures. He certainly appreciated the importance of suitable equipment, capable of taking man to remote, unknown lands.

The caravel was not a completely new ship as it was derived from the carrack, a large ship already in use in the Italian seafaring towns. It was lighter and faster than the carrack and it had more sails and rigging capable of carrying a heavier load.

Originally used for coastal trips, the caravels soon proved to be the most suitable ships for making long voyages and sailing the stormy waters of the Atlantic.

Cross-section of a caravel (below). The caravel was not a completely new ship as it was derived from the carrack, a large ship already in use in the Italian seafaring towns.

When the idea occurred of reaching India from the west

In 1460 Henry the Navigator died without having achieved one of his greatest ambitions: to reach India by sailing round Africa.

The price of spices and other oriental products was very high in Europe because of the cost of transport. They came part of the way by sea, as far as the Red Sea, and then by land, as far as the ports of the Mediterranean.

After the death of Henry the Navigator, pride of place in maritime exploration passed from Portugal to Spain, thanks to the work of the Italian, Christopher Columbus, one of the best remembered men in history.

He was born in Genoa in about the year 1451, a natural sailor, brave and imaginative, who became dedicated to the study of geography and astronomy. Helped and advised by the Florentine geographer, Paolo Toscanelli, he reached a conclusion which was the start of his amazing expedition: if the world is round it must be possible to reach the East by sailing towards the West. Instead of sailing around Africa he decided to cross the Atlantic to reach India.

It was a fortunate geographical error that further convinced Columbus that his idea was right. He thought that the circumference of the Earth was less than we now know it to be.

It is interesting to note that not even after Columbus had discovered America did he realize his mistake, and so he did not suspect that between the point where he landed and the coasts of India there stretched an entire continent and the biggest of the world's oceans.

When Columbus' plan nearly failed

Columbus knocked on every door, trying to find someone who would give him the chance of proving that his theory was right. He was so confident of his brilliant idea and certain of the success of his venture, that he put up with all kinds of humiliations and awkward situations.

At last he seemed to have found somebody prepared to listen to him: Queen Isabella of Spain. She promised to submit his plan for consideration by a special commission of 'learned men and mariners'. This commission made him wait for four years for its decision.

Columbus almost knew what the experts were going to say: they were going to turn him down. Desk scientists are the last to understand expeditions of this kind, Columbus knew, but he waited in hopes for a word from the Queen, even though the committee had already announced its disapproval, as he had feared. But the Queen inexplicably remained silent.

After a long, futile wait, Columbus left for France, disheartened and disillusioned. Suddenly Isabella made up her mind and called him back, just when he was about to cross the border. Three ships were at his disposal, complete with crews and supplies. All they were waiting for was his order to sail.

For Columbus it was the end of a nightmare and the start of the adventure on which he had spent all his time and energy for so many years. His faith in the success of the expedition was unshakeable and in 1492 Columbus started his journey eager for victory.

When Columbus thought he had reached India

The dawn of 3 August 1492 saw three ships lined up in the port of Palos, about to set sail: they were the carrack, the *Santa Maria*, Christopher Columbus' flag-ship, and the two caravels, the *Nina* and the *Pinta*, three ships fit for the most difficult adventures.

The voyage, with its ups and downs, took longer than Columbus had expected.

A month passed with good and bad weather alternating and the sailors showed obvious signs of exhaustion and discontent. They were afraid they would not reach their destination, India, and only their leader's firmness kept them under control.

But, on 9 October, after more than two months at sea, the crews showed a bad sign of their strain: mutiny was being plotted. Columbus pleaded for three more days' time before giving up the expedition. It was enough. Flights of birds appeared and carved sticks and reeds were picked up, bringing the sailors hope. At sunrise on 12 October the long-awaited shout was raised from the crow's-nest of the *Pinta*: land ho!

The silhouette of an unknown land was looming on the horizon. Columbus and all his men were sure they had reached an island off the coast of western India. When other islands were discovered, they called them the 'Indies'.

They could not know that their sea route to India was blocked by a vast mass of land, a land which stretched from the North Pole to the South Pole, a land which would later be known as America.

When Columbus became embittered and disillusioned

Christopher Columbus did not realize he had discovered a new continent but this does not detract from the bravery of his expedition.

On his return to Spain, Columbus was given a royal welcome. He had paved the way to Spanish colonial rule, which was to last for centuries. In the following years Columbus went back to Central America three times. He wanted to find out more about the enormous country he had discovered.

At home, however, the inevitable jealousies, court gossip and the mean ambitions of his rivals had embittered his satisfaction in his achievement. He left for his last expedition in 1502 but returned deeply disillusioned by what he had seen in the conquered lands.

It seemed to him that the natives had been robbed, cheated and, in many cases, massacred by a horde of fanatics driven on solely by their lust for power and wealth. Part of his dream was in ruins, the part in which he had seen himself not as a conqueror but as a civilizer.

When the Europeans reached North America

It was another Italian who landed in North America, this time further north. Like the great Columbus, he was convinced that the shortest way to the East was via the West.

John Cabot was born in Genoa in about 1450 but in 1476 he moved to Venice and became a citizen of that city. About eight year later, he went to London with his family. Henry VII supported him and granted him a contract to sail in search of un-

known lands. This was what the navigator wanted. The English ships, too, were very seaworthy and Cabot, who took his son, Sebastian, with him, came in sight of America at dawn on 24 June 1497.

The place where they landed corresponds to the modern Newfoundland. Cabot's journal describes it as full of white bears and enormous deer. The explorer reports that the inhabitants of that country wore furs and skins and that the sea was teeming with all kinds of fish.

In the same year in which Cabot completed his trip on the North Atlantic route, the Portuguese, Vasco da Gama, made his equally epic voyage on the routes to the south. He rounded the Cape of Good Hope and so opened the direct route to India.

Seldom have so many new and historic discoveries occurred within so short a space of time.

When the name 'America' was first used

After Columbus and Cabot there were countless explorers who probed the coast of America but there was one who gave his name to the new continent: Amerigo Vespucci.

The son of well-to-do parents who lived in Florence, Vespucci started off by studying the classics and then commerce. But he kept the precious fund of geographical knowledge which he had learnt from Paolo Toscanelli, the same scientist who had influenced Columbus' ideas.

Vespucci was a man of strong commonsense who also had a great spirit of adventure and he was able to survive some very difficult moments and dramatic situations. The calm he showed, even in times of extreme danger, has remained famous. Storms at sea and outbreaks of madness left him unruffled and in control of events.

When he got back from his voyages, which he made between 1497 and 1504, at the time of Columbus, he described what he had seen in the minutest detail, with special attention to situations involving people.

Even more than Columbus himself, he was convinced that the new lands were a completely undiscovered continent and he repeated this belief over and over again in his writings.

Perhaps this was the reason why in 1507, a year after the death of Columbus, the German mapmaker, Martin Waldseemüller, suggested that the name 'America', meaning 'Amerigo's land', be given to the new country because it had been so clearly described by Amerigo Vespucci.

Vasco Nuñez de Balboa reached the Isthmus of Darien, the old name for the neck of land between North and South America.

The straits of Magellan

When the Pacific Ocean was discovered

The first person to discover the Pacific Ocean was a Spaniard who landed in America in the wake of the explorer, Rodrigo de Bastidas. His name was Vasco Nuñez de Balboa.

His foresight was as great as his open-mindedness and courage. Remembering the information he had collected from all sides, he pushed down as far as the Isthmus of Darien, the old name for the neck of land between North and South America. After nearly two months of forced march through tropical jungle, he came in sight of the new ocean on 29 September 1513.

The expedition was made possible by the enforced help of 600 natives, under the orders of 200 Spanish soldiers. In the name of the King of Spain, Balboa took possession of the new ocean, calling it the South Sea.

In recognition of this expedition the King appointed Balboa governor under Pedro Arias de Avila. The conqueror's boldness, however, aroused the suspicions of his immediate superior who condemned him to death. But by then the ocean which was to become known universally as the Pacific had been revealed to the world.

When the first European ship entered the Pacific

Another Portuguese renewed the glories of Henry the Navigator: he was the nobleman, Fernão de Magalhães, best known as Magellan. In command of the Spanish fleet, he set off to reach India (Columbus' old dream) by crossing America and then sailing further westwards. He had five ships at his disposal and with them, on 20 September 1519, he headed straight for South America.

He calculated that, by sailing south down the coast of the new continent, he would eventually find a passage through to the ocean which Balboa had first discovered.

The hazards he had to overcome were deadly: in the month of June the *Santiago* was shipwrecked; there were few survivors. The other crews were not always prepared to accept the sacrifices which the situation demanded. When Magellan was almost certain he had finally found the long-sought passage, the *San Antonio* mutinied and sailed back to Spain.

At last the three surviving ships, after difficulties and misadventures of every kind, rounded the tip of South America. An immense but tranquil ocean finally lay before the disheartened seamen and for this very reason the new ocean was called the Pacific.

When the first voyage round the world was completed

The ocean crossing lasted ninety-nine days, from 28 November 1520 to 6 March 1521. But Magellan's hopes and those of his men grew greater and greater as they waited expectantly for India to appear on the horizon.

When supplies were running alarmingly low the three Spanish caravels finally reached the lush islands now called the Philippines.

Here on Mactán Island on 27 April 1521, Magellan was killed in a skirmish with natives.

The expedition continued, although only after one ship, the *Concepcion*, had proved unseaworthy and been burned.

On 6 November 1521 the *Trinidad* and the *Victoria* finally reached the goal of their dreams, India. On 21 December, when the two ships went to set forth again, laden with precious spices, the *Trinidad*, too, turned out to be too rotten to be seaworthy. The *Victoria*, under the command of Elcano, continued alone and alone she carried her men and cargo back to Spain.

On the voyage across the Indian Ocean and round the coast of Africa, scurvy and starvation claimed other victims.

In the end, on 7 September 1522, Elcano brought the leaking but spice-laden ship to anchor off Saville. There were only seventeen other European survivors and four Indians, 'weaker than men have ever been before'. In three years the *Victoria* had sailed round the world, the first ship to do so.

When nautical instruments were improved

Despite the important geographical discoveries of the fifteenth and sixteenth centuries, knowledge of the oceans was still very limited at the end of the eighteenth century.

Scientific progress had brought about some improvements in nautical instruments, however, among which one of the most useful was the sextant. With this it was possible to determine the latitude of a place by measuring the height of the Sun above the horizon. With the building of the Greenwich Royal Observatory in 1675 and the division of the Earth into time zones, working out latitudes became easier. This was a great help to navigation.

When *Terra australis* was discovered

British sea-power made some important contributions to geography and science.

The cartographer, or mapmaker, Captain James Cook, was the leading British navigator of the eighteenth century. He combined a deep knowledge of science with a longing for adventure. Sent by the British Admiralty on a scientific mission to Tahiti in 1769, he asked to be allowed to complete his voyage by exploring the southern hemisphere.

His dream was to discover the great unknown *Terra australis*, or southern continent, of which seafaring folk had spoken and which was supposed to be situated in the southern part of the globe.

On his voyage he found and sailed round the two islands of New Zealand. He then followed the coast of another great country, but without realizing how far it went. It was, in fact, the 'austral' land he had been seeking but, like the Portuguese, Torres, in 1606 and the Dutchman, Jansz, before him, he continued on his way.

The ship in which he was travelling then ran aground on the Great Barrier Reef and it was only with great difficulty that his crew managed to refloat it. It was 1771. The journey quickly came to an end: Cook was disappointed about its main aim, which he thought he had not achieved, but he was comforted by the enormous quantity of scientific and geographical information which he had been able to collect.

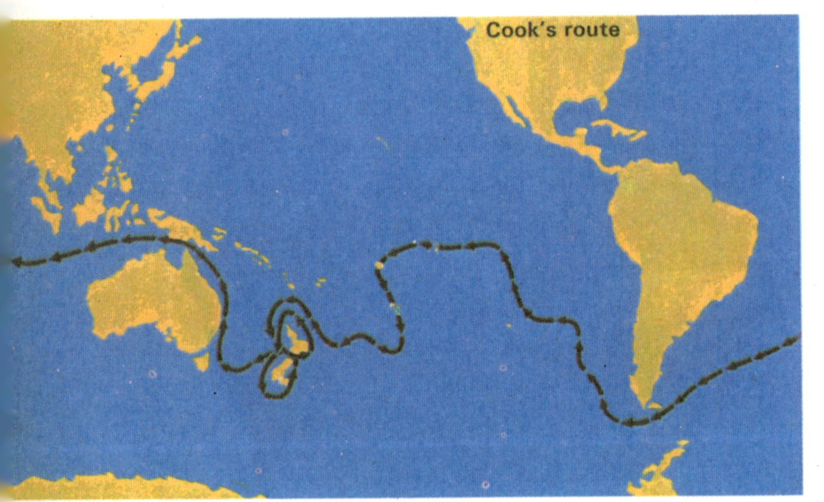

A sextant

When the health of the sailors began to improve

Cook proved to be not only a skilful scientist but also a good organizer. He knew that the success of a sea-voyage depended heavily on the efficiency of the crew and its physical health.

On all his expeditions he put into practice an idea based on patient observations and research. He made the crew eat food which today we would call a balanced diet.

The small number of deaths among the men who accompanied him soon became famous.

The apparent failure of the southern expedition of 1771 remained a secret heartache for Cook. The great navigator organized and carried out three other expeditions to the southern hemisphere, always hoping to discover the huge continent which he had already unwittingly touched on his earlier voyage. No one before him had dared go so far south.

Cook eventually felt compelled to announce that *Terra australis* was non-existent. Of course he had really reached it but had thought it was just another of the many islands of the South Seas.

When Siberia was explored

In 1768 the Empress Catherine the Great of Russia decided to finance an expedition to deepen her country's geographical and scientific knowledge.

Led by the German naturalist, Peter Simon Pallas, the expedition had two main fields of research: Siberia and the vast territories of the Urals and the Altai Mountains. One of its most surprising results was the discovery of an active

ivory tusk trade in Siberia.

The scientists were amazed by this extraordinary business, in a region where there was no sign of an elephant. They eventually found the scientific explanation, however: the ivory tusks belonged to enormous prehistoric mammoths which had lived in the vast expanses of Siberia in the far-off days of the Great Ice Age.

Mungo Park became famous for his journeys down the Niger

Livingstone sees the Victoria Falls for the first time

When the Niger was explored

Europeans had long wanted to explore the interior of Africa. The obstacles in the way were so insurmountable, however, as to discourage any serious attempt. It was not until 1795 that a young Scottish doctor, Mungo Park, agreed to lead an expedition organized by the African Association of England.

The society had been created for scientific and trading purposes but it also hoped to do some good for the natives. The main task entrusted to Mungo Park was to explore the course of the river Niger.

His expedition lasted eighteen months and met with difficulties and dangers of every kind. He only just managed to find his way back to the English trading station at Pisania and then home.

On his return, Park wrote about his adventures in a book, *Travels in the Interior of Africa*, which was published in 1799 and became very popular. After another six years, on 31 January 1805, he set out again for the Gambia, with an even larger party of explorers than had accompanied him in 1795.

He was determined to find the source of the Niger. Very few of his companions reached the banks of the river, however. Out of the forty European members of his expedition, all but eleven were struck down by fatigue and disease.

Park himself was drowned when he was attacked by hostile natives and his boat capsized in the turbulent waters of the Niger. He was not far from the source which he had so doggedly sought.

When Livingstone discovered the Victoria Falls

On 20 November 1840 another Scotsman, the medical missionary David Livingstone, set off to explore Africa. He penetrated into the heart of the Dark Continent, crossing the Kalahari Desert and discovering Lake Ngami and the river Chobe.

In 1852 he sailed a long way up the course of the great Zambesi River, where he was amazed at the grandeur and marvellous beauty of the landscape.

He found a way to fight slavery, which in those days was the 'open sore of the world', as he himself called the slave trade.

For thirty years he did not rest a moment from his religious and medical work. He finally succeeded in crossing Africa, from the Atlantic to the Indian Ocean.

During this expedition he discovered the highest waterfalls in the world, which he named Victoria, after the then Queen of England.

When Stanley found Livingstone

In 1869 the Englishman, Henry Morton Stanley, was sent to Africa by the *New York Herald*. His first task was to search for Livingstone, of whom nothing had been heard for five years. He eventually found him in the village of Ujiji on the west side of Lake Tanganyika, in 1871, and greeted him with the famous words, 'Dr. Livingstone, I presume'.

Stanley then went on methodically to explore the area around the lake. Another epic voyage took him from Lake Victoria to Lake Tanganyika and thence to the Congo.

The newspaper accounts of his travels were followed with great interest all over the world and especially by King of the Belgians, Leopold II. When Stanley returned to Europe in 1878, Leopold persuaded him to work for him towards setting up a Congo Free State under Belgian rule.

Sir Henry Morton Stanley

When Sturt explored Australia

Born in 1795 at Chumar, in India, Charles Sturt felt from his earliest days a strong attraction towards the still unknown continent of Australia. His opportunity came when he was working as a government official and was asked by Sir Ralph Darling, the Governor of New South Wales, to lead a series of expeditions into the Australian interior.

Sturt spent the first three years on careful preparatory excursions, which led him to follow the courses of the rivers Macquarie, Darling and Murray as far as the St. Vincent Gulf, on which the city of Adelaide lies. His real ambition, however, was still to push far into the interior.

At last, in 1844, Sturt set out with fifteen men. They suffered some tremendous hardships during the expedition. After crossing the valley of Cooper's Creek, Sturt succeeded in exploring the terrible stony desert, which today is named after him, and Lake Eyre, the biggest lake in Australia.

When the North Pole was reached

By the beginning of the nineteenth century, attempts to reach the northernmost point of the Earth, the North Pole, had been going on unsuccessfully for several decades. They had frequently ended in tragedy. The American, Robert E. Peary, decided to prepare himself for this venture as carefully as possible. He lived for years with the Eskimos and learned all he could about the region he intended to cross by sled on a journey which was to take many months.

At last the expedition made its base camp near Cape Sheridan in January 1909. Peary had with him 250 dogs for pulling the sleds and about seventy Eskimos. On 22 February he began his historical march in which Peary and a party of five men claimed to have reached the North Pole on 6 April 1909. But to do this, he would have travelled at a much faster speed than any subsequent polar explorer has been able to achieve, and it is unlikely that Peary actually got as far as the Pole. In 1926, Richard Byrd became the first person to reach the North Pole when he flew over it.

When the South Pole was reached

The struggle for the conquest of the South Pole was between the Englishman, Robert Scott, and the Norwegian, Roald Amundsen.

Only a few days apart, they started their march towards the South Pole. It was November 1911, the beginning of the Antarctic spring. The two expeditions took different routes but soon met with difficulties of every kind:

winds of more than 100 kilometres an hour, temperatures more
than 40 degrees below zero,
blizzards and snow-storms.

To all this was added the
problem of carrying enough food
for the five men of each team and
for the animals pulling the sledges.
The journey was all the more
dramatic for the competition between the two parties. They had
to travel fast as even an hour's
delay could lose them their victory.
Amundsen reached the Pole on
14 December 1911, thirty days
ahead of Scott who arrived on
18 January 1912.

Apart from his disappointment
at seeing the Norwegian flag,
Scott was now anxious about
the way back. Many things had
gone badly on the expedition and
the return journey proved to be
disastrous.

Scott lost first one and then
another of his four companions.
When he was only 17 kilometres
away from the base camp and
safety, he pitched his tent to rest
while waiting for a fierce blizzard
to die down. But this tent became
his grave.

When the summit of Everest was reached

Soon after the Second World War
the eyes of all the explorers were
turned to the unconquered summit
of Everest. Numerous expeditions
had failed because they had tackled
the icy wall of its most difficult
face.

The south route was the one to
follow. Sherpa Tenzing had
realized this when taking part in
the Swiss expedition of 1951.

Two years later he joined the
expedition of the English colonel,
Sir John Hunt, whose team also
included the New Zealander, Sir
Edmund Hillary.

The expedition had the advantage of ideal equipment, and helped
by Tenzing's experience a perfect
attack on the summit was planned.
Men and machines at last over-
came the tremendous forces of
nature.

At eleven thirty in the morning
of 29 May 1953, Hillary and
Tenzing reached the 'roof of the
world' and surveyed the breath-
taking spectacle of the gigantic
Himalayas at their feet.

When man began to study the stars

Why does the Sun rise and set? Why does the Moon appear in so many shapes in the sky? Why do some stars look brighter than others? To these and many other questions man tried to find the answers, often mixing scientific facts with fanciful beliefs.

The beneficial effects of the Sun, for example, were thought to be so miraculous that they made primitive man believe in it as a god. The Egyptians and the Aztecs are outstanding among the peoples who worshipped the Sun, dedicating colossal temples to this, their greatest god.

Apart from religious and mythological beliefs, the earliest known studies of the stars date back to 3,000 years before Christ. The first accounts of unusual astronomical events (such as eclipses of the Sun and the Moon) were made then.

It was the Greeks, however, with Eratosthenes and Hipparchus, who first tried to give a scientific explanation to the astronomical happenings of their time. Their theories were taken as the basis of all subsequent astronomical research, which Ptolemy summarized in his *Almagest* (the Arabic word for 'the greatest') in the second century A.D.

According to these theories, the Earth is in the centre of the Universe with the planets and the stars rotating around it in circular orbits. This belief is known as geocentrism.

When Ptolemy's idea of the Universe collapsed

Ptolemy's theory was regarded as perfect and indestructible until, nearly twelve centuries later, the great Nikolai Kopernik, known to us as Copernicus (1473–1543), reached the opposite conclusion. From his studies of the motion of the planets he decided that the centre of the Universe was the Sun and that the planets, including the Earth, move round it.

The Polish scientist could not announce his discoveries because they clashed with the official view and he was afraid of persecution. So the new idea was not published until after his death.

Known as the theory of heliocentrism, referring to the Sun as the centre, it was not developed further until the beginning of the seventeenth century, when the German, Johannes Kepler (Keplerus), confirmed it with his three famous laws of planetary motion.

The Italian, Galileo Galilei, then proved the theory scientifically with the use of the recently invented telescope. All these ideas were crowned by the English scientist, Sir Isaac Newton (1642–1727), who discovered the law of gravity, which explains why the planets are bound to rotate round the Sun and cannot drift away from it.

Sundial

Aztec temple to the sun-god 104

When radio astronomy began

A new science, perhaps the youngest of all, is radio astronomy. With its help it is easier to understand not only the evolution of the Universe but also the very nature of our own planet.

The father of this new science is generally considered to be Karl Jansky, an American engineer. In 1931 he discovered that the signals on a 14·6 metre wavelength came from a precise point in the sky, in the area of the Sagittarius constellation.

In 1936, an American radio amateur, Grote Reber, using Jansky's directions, started to explore the sky, carefully noting the origin of the signals. The instrument he used was a parabolic dish nearly 10 metres in diameter, which may be said to be the first radio telescope.

Today there are radio telescopes with parabolic reflectors of 50 metres and more in diameter, capable of exploring the Universe thousands of millions of light years away. The telescope at Jodrell Bank measures 76 metres in diameter and was the first fully steerable radio telescope.

When the race to the Moon began

After so many conquests on Earth, man felt ready to conquer space. In this exciting and dangerous race, the boldness of the competitors was no longer sufficient. They had to be backed by the careful preparations of thousands of highly specialized people.

From now on it will become more and more necessary for the whole of mankind to unite all its energies if the exploration of space is to be successful. Proof of this is the race to the Moon, which has involved Russians and Americans in high-level competition.

On 4 October 1957 the U.S.S.R. launched the first of Earth's artificial satellites, the *Sputnik* (or 'fellow traveller').

Four months later, the first American satellite, *Explorer I,* discovered the Van Allen radiation belt above the Earth.

More than three years passed before, on 12 April 1961, the first man was launched into space. He was the Russian, Yuri Gagarin, who made a complete orbit of the Earth in 89·34 minutes.

On 20 February 1962 the first

Two of Galileo's telescopes

United States astronaut, John Glenn, was put into orbit. In June 1963 the first woman cosmonaut, Valentina Tereshkova, went into

Yuri Gagarin

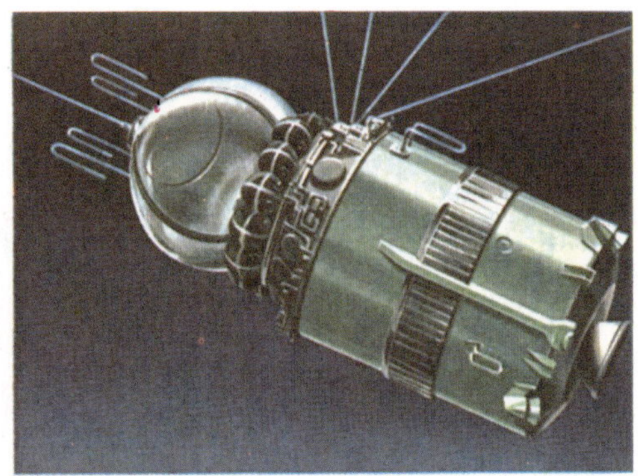

The spaceship _Vostok_

The telescope at Jodrell Bank

orbit with her _Vostok 6_, two days after the _Vostok 5_.

Another two and a half years of feverish preparation passed and, on the 15 December 1965, two American spaceships rendezvoused in space, flying together for six hours: they were _Gemini 6_ and 7.

In January 1969 two Soviet spacecraft, the _Soyuz 4_ and _5_, linked up in flight and, for the first time, two astronauts changed from one spacecraft to the other.

When the exploration of the Moon began

The success of the Americans in the race to conquer the Moon was given a decisive boost by the launching of _Apollo 9_ in March 1969. It was then that the lunar module, the vehicle designed to carry the astronauts on the lunar soil, was tried out. The practice run for the landing on the Moon was entrusted to _Apollo 10,_ which gave the astronauts Stafford and Cernan the chance to fly over the surface of the Moon in the lunar module.

The attention of the whole world was then turned to Cape Kennedy: and on the 16 July 1969 the American astronauts, Armstrong, Aldrin and Collins, left in the spaceship _Apollo 11_ for the big expedition. After three days of perfect flight, on 17, 18 and 19 July, the lunar module broke loose from the command module with Armstrong and Aldrin on board and, at 9.20 p.m., it made a perfect landing on lunar soil.

At 3.56 a.m. on 20 July, Armstrong became the first creature from Earth to set foot on the Moon. The goal which had seemed such folly had been achieved.

When other inhabitants of the Universe may be discovered

Astronomical research increases with all the new scientific instruments which are always being invented. Nowadays some very powerful telescopes are used to study the sky.

The telescope at Zelenchukskaya in Russia, for example, is world-famous for its huge reflector 6 metres in diameter. Radio telescopes have also greatly extended the field of research into the Universe.

The Universe consists of countless other stars similar to the Sun, around which other planets and satellites often move, just as in our solar system.

The similarities between our solar system and other distant systems of stars are amazing. That is why the last great question which man has to ask is, perhaps, the most fascinating of all: do other beings like us exist on any of the countless worlds which fill the sky? And if they do exist, will we be able to communicate with them and find out how they live?

Though there would be enormous difficulties in finding common ground with the cultures of the other inhabitants of the universe, they would be overcome.

It is unlikely that we would be able to exchange literary information with them, but there are certain elementary ideas which must be understandable to any creature that has developed the apparatus needed to receive our radio messages. For instance, the theorem of Pythagoras would be easy to transmit and would be readily understood.

Experiments along these lines are already being carried out.

WHEN POWER BEGAN

Today we are always hearing about 'power': electric power, mechanical power, nuclear power. But, although the word seems so modern, it is in fact very ancient, going back to the dawn of man. The only kind of power known to primitive man was that of his own muscles. It was with the strength of their muscles alone that our distant ancestors struggled for what they needed to live and to gain the mastery over nature and the animals.

Soon man discovered that the power he had been given could be increased by special tools: a piece of wood or bone or a pointed stone were better weapons than his bare hands.

In fact one of the main characteristics of man as opposed to the less advanced animals is the ability to put natural materials to precise uses.

Most things that are made are tools or weapons, and they are fashioned in order to make up for man's physical deficiencies. They have played an enormously important part in the evolutionary process. With such instruments man found it much easier to kill his prey.

When primitive man then became a hunter of fast-moving animals and birds, he discovered the spear-thrower and the bow and arrow. These made him feel stronger and better able to secure the food he needed.

Spear-throwers and arrows were man's first real weapons. They marked an important stage in his development. The spear-thrower was a piece of wood with a hook in which a spear was engaged so that it could be thrown with much greater force. It was a kind of continuation of the human arm, a kind of catapult. A weapon very similar to the primitive spear-thrower is still used today by the Australian aborigines.

It was only with the bow and arrow, however, that man became a true hunter. He grew to be such an expert with this weapon that he could hit birds in flight and fishes swimming in the water. The rapid progress which man made after the discovery of these weapons shows how important they were to his evolution.

In particular, through them our ancestors became more aware of the muscular power they had been given. Although strengthened by their weapons, it still remained their chief force.

When animal power began to be used

Some time between 8000 and 5000 B.C. that is, in the Neolithic Age, students of the history of man tell us that he began not only to kill animals but also to breed them.

For thousands of years he had been hunting animals, some of them much larger and stronger than he was, to feed himself and obtain their skins. Now he had realized that it was better to make friends with them and put them to other uses, instead of always catching and killing them.

The first animals which man domesticated were probably the ones he needed for food. Quite soon, however, he learned to domesticate other, bigger animals which could help him till the fields.

The animals have helped tremendously in human activities.

Think, for example, of the many services they have carried out for farmers over the centuries: from ploughing to sowing, from watering the land to clearing it of trees, they have worked side by side with man.

Ancient horse-drawn 'locomotive': the horse walked on a moving track

When man began to use the forces of nature

Man had found his first urge to progress in the basic need to survive. As his life gradually became free of the burden of hunger, he began to take note of his surroundings.

Many of the things which he had discovered out of necessity were thus enriched by many others which he discovered out of curiosity.

For example, what was it that drove primitive man to move away from the place where he was born? What made him venture forth on the treacherous waters of the rivers and seas? What made him use the mysterious, powerful forces which nature had to offer? It was partly need but also curiosity, the two big incentives which have spurred on the progress of man in every age.

When man discovered the force of the wind

Exactly when the wind was first used by man for his own ends is uncertain but it may have happened at the beginning of the Neolithic Age.

In 1929 the archaeologist, Sir Flinders Petrie, excavating at Al Fayyum in Egypt, found a stone model of a sailing boat which he claimed had been made a good eleven thousand years before.

Sailing ships became widely used until, in the eighteenth century, they reached the height of their splendour. With their huge sails spread to the wind, they caught as much of it as possible and so were blown along at high speed.

The date when the first windmill made its appearance is also uncertain but it was probably introduced into Europe in the twelfth century. Windmills became increasingly widespread until the early nineteenth century when the development of steam power caused their slow decline.

The windmills of Holland are the most celebrated of all.

When man began to use solar energy

The Sun's energy, which gives life to all the creatures on Earth, is perhaps the one kind of energy which man has not yet learned to harness properly. Even in the field of bodily health, it is only in the last few decades that medicine has discovered how to use the health-giving powers of the Sun's rays for treating certain diseases.

If we remember that the Sun is emitting an astonishing amount of energy all the time, so much that it is quite beyond our grasp, and

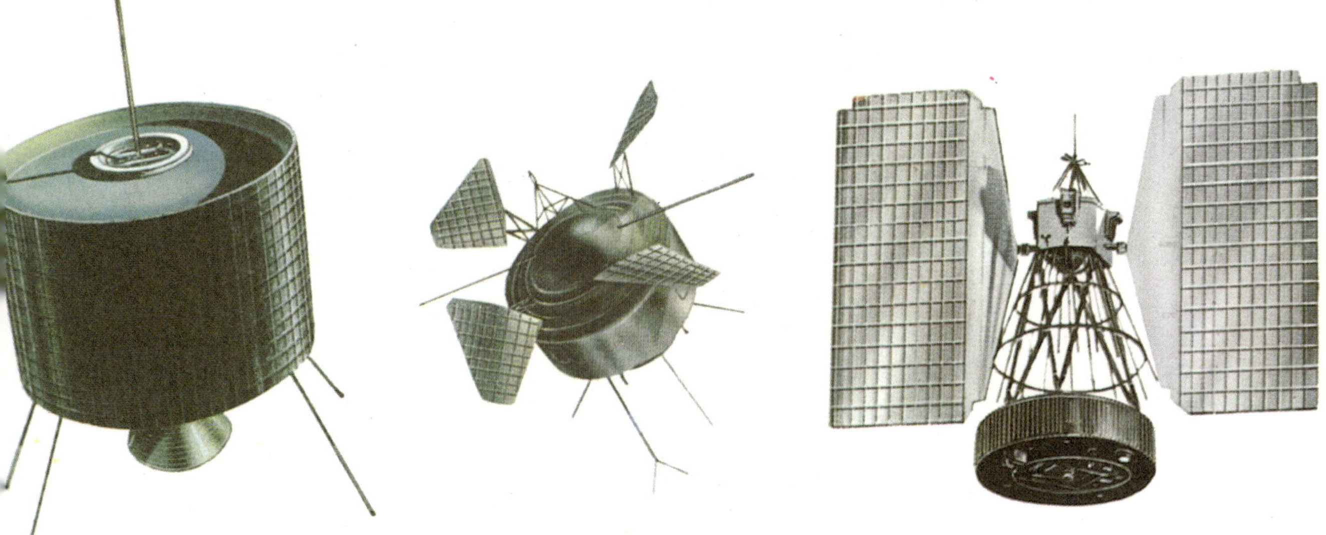

Early Bird, the first commercial communications satellite (left). The gigantic Russian satellite *Proton* (centre) The *Nimbus* (U.S.A.) (right)

that life about us is thriving because of it, we will have some idea of its potential uses.

Some very complex devices are already being worked by solar energy. There are, for example, the Orbiting Solar Observatories (O.S.O.) with special solar cells on their outsides to produce electric power. Other similar devices are mounted on space exploration equipment.

Or there is the solar furnace, consisting of a series of reflective mirrors to produce electricity from the heat of the Sun. The largest example of this is Solar One, the 10-megawatt solar power plant in California.

A recent invention is the electric car, operated by batteries charged by the mains power supply.

Electric vehicles are nothing new: they were used for the first time a century ago, and the first practical use of them dates from about 1900.

Among their obvious advantages is their silent running and the absence of fumes that pollute the atmosphere.

When man began to use the water of the rivers

The greatest civilizations grew up on the banks of rivers. Their water provided drink for men and animals and irrigated the fields.

River water was therefore used first of all to sustain life. Then man soon learned how to sail on the rivers, following the current. Even today, in densely wooded countries, lumberjacks use the currents

The train was invented in the nineteenth century. To the more old-fashioned it seemed an invention of the devil, destined to be very short-lived, but in fact it revolutionized the entire world of transport. Even today trains pulled by steam engines are still in use.

With the invention of electric power, industry was quickly radically transformed. Machines hitherto worked by steam were now worked by electricity.

to carry timber to the sawmill or port.

But the water of the rivers was a source of power which was to be more widely used. As soon as man invented the millstone he realized that the flow of the rivers could turn the millstones faster than a man or animal could by its own strength. Until quite recently nearly all rivers had their own watermills.

There was one point, at its falls, where the current became even stronger. There nothing could stop the rushing waters as they hurtled down with a deafening roar.

Yet, once again, man managed to find a way of harnessing this force. When the tranquil flow of the rivers was no longer sufficient to set his inventions going, the violent force of the waterfalls had to be called upon. Even today much of our electric power is produced by the water of waterfalls. Where there are no natural falls we build them artifically with weirs and dams.

When steam power was discovered

If we had to put an exact date on the beginning of the age of modern progress, we might well take 1690. This was the year in which Denis Papin put forward his conclusions on the study of water vapour in his thesis known as the *Acts of Leipzig*. His boiler, which he called a steam digester, was the mother of all the steam engines later used for converting the force of vaporized water into movement.

The use of hydrothermal power, that is power produced by super-heated water, made rapid, successful progress. Steam power was one of the main causes of the

Industrial Revolution of the eighteenth century. Steam-driven looms gave rise to the first industrial boom of our times.

It was not until the nineteenth century, however, that the more ingenious use of steam gave birth to the train. To the more old-fashioned it seemed an invention of the devil, destined to be very short-lived, but in fact it revolutionized the entire world of transport.

Steam engines were in universal use for over 100 years, but after the Second World War, they dwindled in favour of diesel and electric traction. They are still used to a limited extent in some European countries but are rare in mainline service.

The power obtained by heating water was so great that sea transport, as well as land transport, was soon driven by special steam boilers. These turned enormous paddles, like watermill wheels, which propelled the ship along. The old Mississipi paddle-steamers which were a major form of transport on that river during the nineteenth century, are still famous.

When the power of the sea was harnessed

The sea is a deep, largely unexplored mine full of riches. The surprises in store for us in the future must be quite fantastic, considering that oil, gas, diamonds, cobalt, and manganese all abound in the sea.

The force of the tides is already being used to produce electric power. A famous example of this is the wave-power electricity generating station on the estuary of the river Rance in Brittany, France. It was opened on 26 November 1966 and is capable of producing 544 million kilowatt hours a year. The use of the temperature of sea currents to produce other types of power seems near at last.

Fresh water, however, is in short supply, acutely so in some places. This has led scientists to design and build plant for taking the salt out of sea water and so turn it into fresh water for drinking or industrial purposes.

In these days of the use of natural power, we look to the sea as one of our riches.

When electric power was discovered

Today we think nothing of pressing a switch and brightening our lives with warm light, turning a knob and watching a television show, moving a lever and starting up a whole factory. All this is made possible by a powerful and beneficial source of energy which we call electricity.

Not two centuries have passed since the discovery of Count Alessandro Volta who, with his battery, gave birth to the age of electricity in 1801. Yet electricity has become the indispensable force which makes the world go round.

The New Yorkers became only too aware of this when, on 9 and 10 November 1965, a city-wide black-out threatened their whole way of life.

The need for electricity is increasing rapidly and is used as a yardstick for the development of a community. But the production of electricity is meeting grave difficulties because the thermal variety poisons the environment, the hydro type has already expanded as far as it can go, and the nuclear sort has problems of waste disposal.

When electrical energy was first used

One way of producing electricity is in generating stations operated by the force of water moving enormous turbines, or rotary motors. When connected to generators, they produce electric current.

Another kind of generating station is the thermoelectric station. Instead of the force of water it uses the force of heat produced by fuels like oil, coal or gas. This kind of generating station is on the increase because of the present shortage of water to feed hydroelectric stations. Tides are now being used to generate electricity, too.

The two essential pieces of equipment in a generating station are the turbine and the generator. The turbine is set going by the action of falling water or by steam produced by burning fuel.

It then starts up a movement in the generator which converts this movement into electric current. The size of the turbines and generators varies according to the production capacity of each generating station.

Electric power is certainly the chief source of power in the twentieth century. We find it everywhere: there is not a machine which is not operated, directly or indirectly, by electricity. The production and consumption of this type of power is increasing at a tremendous rate.

For a rough idea of how much electric power is needed at the moment, we only have to realize that it takes one kilowatt of electricity to wash a few kilos of clothes in a washing machine but it takes a good 375 kilowatts to make a ton of steel and as much as 15,000 kilowatts to make a ton of aluminium.

Generating capacity in Europe amounts to more than 500,000 megawatts, about a quarter of world capacity, which increased from about 1 million to 2 million megawatts in the 1970s.

Capacity has risen at this rate to match consumption and it will have to grow just as fast, otherwise all human life will be thwarted by the inability to expand.

As the hydroelectric stations are inadequate, however hard they work, and the thermoelectric stations need coal and oil, supplies of which are slowly being exhausted, it is essential to find other sources of energy for making electricity.

The water collected in a reservoir is carried to its destination through various sizes of pipe. Similarly, electricity is carried by special copper cables which conduct a greater or lesser amount of power, depending on their thickness.

The huge cables are held up by pyramid-shaped framed steel pylons and the thinner lines supported by wooden or cement poles. Even thinner wires form the electrical circuits in our houses. As water runs from the biggest pipe into the smallest, so electricity is transmitted from the thickest cable to the thinnest.

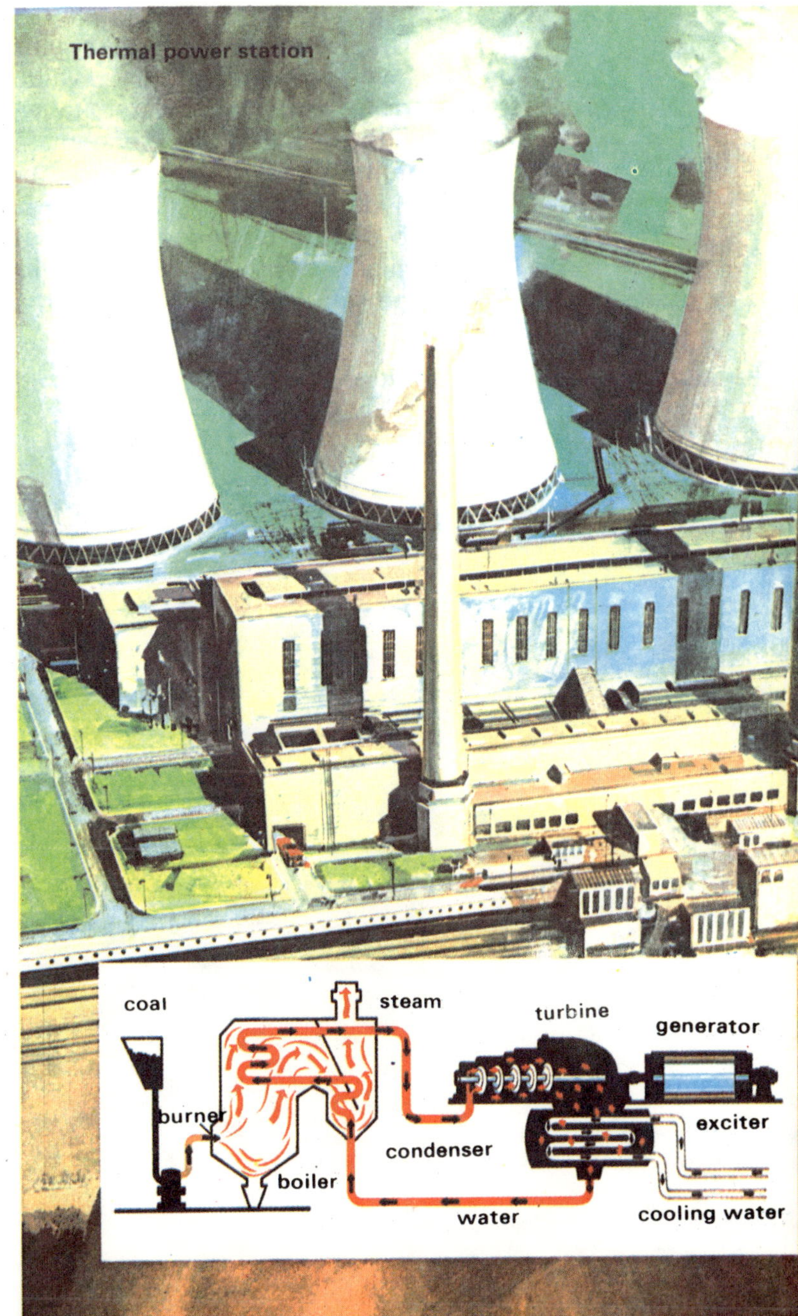

When electricity began to be used in industry

With the invention of electric power, industry was quickly transformed. Machines worked by steam were now worked by electricity. It saved time and was more practical and economical. Steam boilers were slowly replaced, although they remained the undisputed leaders in the field of transport: the electric train was still a long way off.

The invention of the hydraulic, or water-driven turbine, which made for better use of water power, was the work of the Frenchman, Benoît Fourneyron, in 1827.

Hydraulic turbines reached a high degree of perfection and it became possible to produce as much as 90 per cent of the theoretical maximum amount of power.

When the turbine came to be connected to direct current generators (dynamos) or alternating current generators (alternators), more electricity was produced more cheaply.

If we compare the earliest generators with the extremely powerful, sometimes colossal dynamos of the modern electricity stations, we will see how much progress has been made in this field, which is one of the most important industries of the present day.

When drilling for oil began

It seems certain that oil has been known about since the earliest times and that the most advanced peoples, like the Chinese, for example, used it in the normal way for lighting their homes.

It was only at the beginning of the nineteenth century, however, that scientists and technologists started seriously to investigate the use of oil as a source of power. The experiments proved that it was possible and oil was forecast as an indispensable source of energy in the very near future. Nearly all the oil which had been used up until then had been from natural outcrops on the surface but drilling for oil under the ground now began.

The first drilling took place on 27 August 1859 at Titusville, Pennsylvania, in the United States, when a 21-metre well was drilled. It was directed by Colonel Edwin Drake, a pioneer in oil prospecting in America. With the successful discovery of oil the area boomed and the first oil refinery was also built at Titusville.

High-speed 150 megawatt generator rotor (above)

50 megawatt generator stator (below)

When the internal combustion engine was invented

One invention destined to succeed was the internal combustion engine. In engines of this type, a fuel-air mixture is burned so that the hot gases produced exert a force on moving parts of the machine.

In the last years of the nineteenth century many attempts had been made to develop an engine of this type. Above all, it was the work of Lenoir, Schmidt, Beau de Rochas and Daimler which brought about the internal combustion engine, the father of all the millions of vehicles now travelling on the roads of the world, propelled by the same device.

Oil was used to run the new engine right from the start. If supplies of this precious liquid were to cease today, many of our activities would stop at once. The discovery of more and more petroleum deposits has therefore become a problem which concerns all the countries in the world.

When the use of petroleum spread

The rapid acceptance and spread of the internal combustion engine, particularly at the beginning of this century, made it all the more necessary quickly to increase the exploitation of existing petroleum deposits and find new ones.

The problem of transporting the crude oil, as petroleum in its natural state is called, from the wells to the refineries became more and more critical, too.

It is in the refineries that petroleum is transformed into liquids more suitable for fuels: petrol for cars and aeroplanes, liquid gases such as butane and propane, lubricating oil for engines, diesel oil and naphtha, used for heating.

One of the most recent developments is that of providing protein for use in animal feedstuffs.

Oil deposits are scattered over the surface of the Earth so the crude oil has to be transported in a variety of ways. The most common are road, rail or ocean tankers and pipelines.

Oil tankers of up to about 500,000 tons are the largest vessels in use in the world. They are known as V.L.C.C.s (very large crude carriers).

Pipelines are the most recent method and the most likely to be used in the future as it is the most practical and fastest.

It is only in the last few decades that deposits of natural gas have been discovered in

Electric car

Europe. This is used both for domestic purposes, such as heating, and as a fuel, instead of oil, in many industries.

Both natural gas and oil are precious sources of energy and those countries which are fortunate enough to possess large reserves are assured of their future energy supplies. Britain has reserves of oil and gas in the North Sea as well as on land.

When nuclear power was discovered

Nuclear power is entirely the result of highly scientific research. With the splitting of the atom at the beginning of the twentieth century, it became possible to set off reactions which produce a powerful supply of energy. If not properly channelled, however, this energy can prove lethal to man. It is therefore true to say that the most recent of the sources of power discovered by man is by far the strongest.

This immense force, which made its first unhappy appearance during the Second World War, today has peaceful applications of far-reaching importance. It is used both in medicine and in transport, in industry and in daily life.

Nuclear-powered ships, for example, can sail long distances without needing to refuel, a useful requirement in icebreakers and aircraft carriers. Space probes that voyage far from the Sun are powered by miniature nuclear reactors, and the radioactivity of materials produced by nuclear reactors is valuable in science, medicine and industry.

In the field of agriculture, radioactivity can help make some important discoveries about plant foods and the use of different types of soil and fertilizer.

If radioactivity, that is the force released by an atom when its nucleus is split in two, can be controlled and harnessed by man for purposes of peaceful progress, it will prove to be an incomparable source of energy and a power for good.

But tragedies like the atomic bombing of Hiroshima and Nagasaki when hundreds of thousands of people were killed in Japan in August 1945 must not be repeated.

When atomic power was used for producing electricity

A practical application of nuclear power for peaceful purposes is the production of electricity. Since the late 1940s, the years immediately after the Second World War, scientists and technologists have managed to develop equipment for producing electric power from nuclear energy.

The first atomic power station in the world was built in 1956 at Calder Hall in Cumberland. The plant's present output is 180

megawatts, or 180 million watts, of electricity.

Since then, nuclear power has spread around the world. It now provides about 8 per cent of the world's generating capacity, having expanded ten times during the 1970s. The countries today with the greatest nuclear generating capacity are the United States, France, Japan and Russia, followed by West Germany, Britain, Sweden and Canada.

The world's natural fuel resources such as coal and oil, now used to generate electricity, may well be exhausted in about 100 to 200 years. However it is estimated that the resources of nuclear power are approximately 100 times as large as the energy available from existing fuel reserves.

It is hard to predict exactly what technological and scientific developments will be brought about by the use of nuclear power. We can, however, take a quick look at some of the more extraordinary aspects of an invention which will certainly change the face of the Earth.

At Farsta, on the edge of Stockholm, the whole town's heating is provided by one nuclear reactor. In the nuclear power station at Chinon, in France, as much electricity is produced by a ton of uranium as is produced by 10,000 tons of coal. This is only considered a modest achievement, however, for the same quantity of uranium can in fact produce three times as much electricity. In the not-too-distant future 'rapid neutron' reactors will be able to achieve some really staggering results. A ton of atomic fuel will produce as much power as is obtained by burning 600,000 tons of coal.

In the field of propulsion, nuclear-powered ships and submarines have already been tried. The largest aircraft carriers are equipped with nuclear reactors, which render them completely self-sufficient. Nuclear submarines can stay submerged for months on end and quickly change their position, which makes them more useful and independent.

In the field of space travel, distant space probes such as the *Voyager 2* probe that is exploring the outer planets are nuclear powered. This is because these spacecraft travel too far from the Sun to be able to use solar cells.

The first nuclear reactor at Chicago (above)
Calder Hall: the first atomic power station (below)

WHEN INVENTING BEGAN

Our daily lives could not proceed normally without the valuable help of metals.

Copper was one of the earliest metals used by man. Implements and weapons dating from 5000 B.C. have been found in graves in Egypt. There are also records of the working of copper mines on the Sinai Peninsula in about 3800 B.C. It took more than a thousand years for the appreciation and application of copper to spread through Europe. Few inventions can have been as important as this great discovery of our ancestors.

Man soon learned how to make copper harder by alloying it, or mixing it, with tin, so producing bronze. It is the discovery of bronze (5,000 years ago) that is generally said to mark the beginning of the history of modern man.

With the discovery of metals, man had taken a big step forward towards civilization. His evolution naturally progressed more rapidly from then on. At first little bronze was used but by the late Bronze Age there was a great development in the use of metals for tools, weapons, utensils, shields, trumpets and coins. These were shaped by the blacksmith, who soon became surrounded with mystery by his fellowmen.

To their minds, anyone capable of drawing these marvels out of the fire must surely be a kind of wizard blessed with supernatural powers. Yet, despite the belief that his art was magic, the blacksmith was really just a skilful, intelligent craftsman who knew how to master the forces which nature put at his disposal.

Even thousands of years later, when the blacksmith had become a familiar and commonplace figure, he still aroused a feeling of respect and wonder in the unskilled layman.

Today the iron and steel works continue the ancient art of ironworking on an industrial scale. Using very advanced techniques, they achieve some amazing results.

When cast iron and steel were obtained

Cast iron, a mixture of iron and carbon, has occupied a position of great importance in the industrial world since the eighteenth century. It was in this century too, in 1740, that Benjamin Huntsman produced steel at Sheffield and the modern age of metals began. The production of steel involves close control of the amount of carbon present with the iron.

Both cast iron and steel are produced in blast-furnaces, which are quickly becoming fully automated units.

The blast-furnace, with its chimney stack 35 to 40 metres high, is filled with layers of coke and iron ore. The very high firing temperature, of between 1,600 and 1,800 degrees, produces cast iron which is, in fact, a compound of iron and carbon.

Steel, too, is a compound of iron and carbon but the amount of carbon it contains must not be more than 1·7 per cent.

When aluminium was isolated

The most plentiful metal in the Earth's crust is aluminium, although until a century ago no one knew of its existence. This is because aluminium does not exist in the pure state, like gold, but is always combined with other minerals, such as bauxite and kaolin. Aluminium was first discovered by Sir Humphrey Davy in 1807 and first produced in 1827 by Hans Christian Oersted. Afterwards Wöhler improved on Oersted's methods and succeeded in obtaining the metal in a purer form.

Today aluminium is used in the manufacture of all kinds of

tools and vehicles, from kitchen utensils and electric wires to train, car and aircraft parts, as it is the basic ingredient in the light alloys or metal mixtures, from which they are made.

The manuscript of Walter de Milemete shows a cannon, probably brass, at the moment of firing (above)

Soon the black powder, which made such terrifying explosions, spread all over the world. It revolutionized the methods of war and became a constant source of evil, although it also found some extremely useful peaceful applications.

(From top) Soldier with a hand cannon mounted on a bar; old hand firearms of crude iron, brass and a mortar

When gunpowder was discovered

It is impossible to say exactly when gunpowder was discovered. Some say that it was being used in China as long ago as the eleventh century to power rockets and fire crude guns.

It was not until the fourteenth century that there was any definite knowledge of it in Europe, however, but the origin of this invention is uncertain as several cities claim to be its birthplace.

The best known of the possible inventors of gunpowder is a certain fourteenth-century German, Friar Berthold of Freiburg, to whom the city has dedicated a statue.

This monk, carrying out experiments in his laboratory, is supposed to have discovered the make-up of gunpowder by chance. A stray spark is said to have set fire to the mixture he had prepared, and the resulting explosion sent the pestle flying out of his hand.

Gunpowder was actually first introduced by the Arabs, who had learned how to use it from the peoples of the East, where they travelled as traders.

When the first rockets were invented

Today we often see or hear of a manned-rocket being launched into space. The first rockets, however, simple though they were, were invented in China and were mainly used for entertaining the crowds at all the religious ceremonies which filled the Chinese calendar.

It is said that when the Chinese city of Tzu T'ung was besieged by a powerful enemy army in the year A.D. 994, the first rockets designed for military purposes were used. Although this may only be a story, it is a fact that by the thirteenth century rockets were being used in China, propelled by the black powder later known as gunpowder.

Even proper batteries were used for launching volleys of rockets all at once, very like those used in the modern armies.

The rocket came to Europe from the Middle East and was used for amusement and in war.

When the 'black powder' was replaced by more powerful explosives

The need for more powerful weapons for their armies has spurred all the countries in the world to continue to find new, more efficient explosives.

After gunpowder, man discovered dynamite, nitrogelatine, trinitrotoluene (T.N.T.) and guncotton. Of course they have not always been used for military purposes. Explosives are used in mines where coal or other minerals are being dug, for tunnelling through mountains and in all kinds of other excavating work, instead of or as well as human labour.

The first rockets were invented in China (above)

The American Robert Goddard used a hearse to tow his rockets to the launching tower (below)

In the two World Wars of this century, weapon design changed completely. Long-range guns, high explosives for armour-piercing charges, liquid-propellent rockets like the German V1 and V2, all played dramatic parts in the battles.

These rockets led to the later development of huge, intercontinental ballistic missiles which can be used to reach every part of the world.

Despite the peace initiatives on all sides, it seems that war will never be completely over, which is why more and more powerful weapons are still being built.

Only when man succeeds in using the force of explosives for peace alone, can he claim to have made a really worthwhile contribution to his own progress.

When the telescope was invented

It was 1609 when Galileo Galilei, Professor of Mathematics at the University of Padua, heard about the invention of the telescope by a Dutch spectacle-maker. By putting one lens on top of another he had discovered that the objects at which he was looking seemed bigger. Galileo decided to build a telescope for himself. Although

(Above) fragment from Hero's Pneumatics, published in Urbino in 1575. (Below) part of Villard's rope mechanism

small, his instrument enabled him to see the mountains and craters of the Moon, the spots on the Sun and the satellites of Jupiter. He also established that the Milky Way is nothing but a collection of myriads of stars.

In fact, although the telescope was invented by the Dutch spectacle-maker, Galileo was the first to use this wonderful instrument for scientific purposes. He therefore deserves his reputation as one of the inventors of the telescope, the instrument for 'seeing at a distance'.

Galileo's first telescopes, treasured as priceless antiques, are preserved in the Galileo Museum at Florence.

When Leonardo da Vinci designed his amazing machines

Since the earliest times man has done his best to invent labour-saving machines.

It was only with the many-sided genius of Leonardo da Vinci, however, that plans were made for revolutionary machines which are quite amazing in the way they anticipate modern devices.

Leonardo's projects included a machine gun and numerous other pieces of military equipment; a helicopter worked by a spring called an airscrew; very light bridges; even parachutes and boats with paddle-wheels. His inventions were not just drawings in his notebooks. He completed the construction of the canal at Martesana and two other important navigation and irrigation canals, the Naviglio Grande and the Naviglio Interno. He also designed musical instruments, such as lyres and violas.

When printing was invented

It is true that the Chinese had already 'printed' a book in A.D. 868, but the invention of printing as we know it was made in Europe in the 1450s.

Many people claimed to be the originators of the movable type from which books are printed. The invention is generally attributed to Johann Gutenberg, however, a master craftsman of Mainz on the river Rhine, in Germany.

The first type used by Gutenberg was made of wood and his printing presses were worked by hand. Today, automatic printing machines can run off thousands of books in a few minutes.

When the first clocks were made

Even people who had no form of writing had their own special way of noting the succession of the days, the seasons and the years. Among the earliest instruments used for measuring time were sundials, sand-glasses and water-clocks.

The clock as we know it did not appear until the end of the thirteenth century. Before that the Arabs had built devices similar to the clock but not as efficient.

The first clocks were enormous and were nearly always placed on church or bell-towers so that everyone in the town could see them. Their movements were simple and noisy but they worked for many years, although they did not always tell the correct time.

The earliest English turret clocks still in existence were installed at Salisbury Cathedral, Wells Cathedral and Dover Castle.

When the first reflecting telescope was invented

After the first scientific telescopes of Galileo, the study and design of instruments for exploring the mysteries of the Universe made steady progress.

The first reflecting telescope to be built was Sir Isaac Newton's. It was 1671 when he developed this special new instrument in which light was reflected by a concave (curved inward) mirror

A very early wooden-frame chamber clock, dated 1643

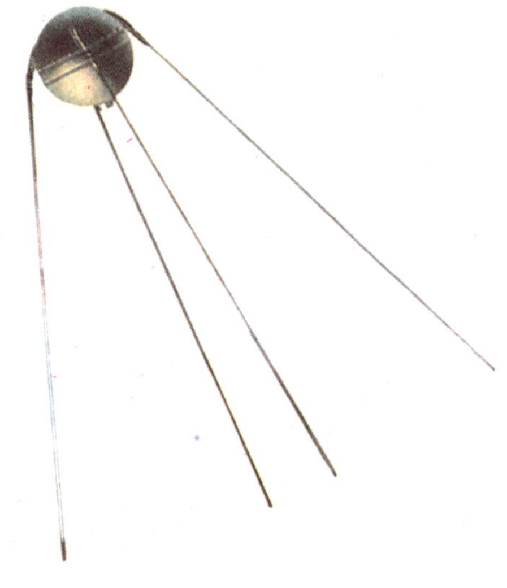

The Russian satellite *Sputnik I,* Earth's first artificial satellite

within the focus of the main mirror. The image produced was observed on an eyepiece at the side of the telescope. Newton preferred using a reflecting telescope because it was free of the coloured fringes which nearly always make images in refracting telescopes look blurred or out-of-focus.

Because it is so easy to use and so cheap, the Newtonian type of reflecting telescope is still widely used today.

When the first large telescope was built

In 1947 an enormous mirror was carried up to the top of Mount Palomar in California. It was the essential part of what was then the largest telescope in the world. It has a diameter of 5 metres and weighs about 15 tons.

Making such a large mirror presented some almost insurmountable problems, as the pure quartz which it had been intended to use lost its brightness and smoothness when it cooled. It was decided to use Pyrex, which took a whole year to cool in perfect conditions. The polishing alone took another eleven years, by the end of which only 15 out of the original 20 tons were left which shows the enormous amount of high precision work entailed.

Visitors to the telescope are kept at a safe distance, because just the heat of their bodies could upset the balance and accuracy of this complex and sensitive apparatus.

When radio astronomy became important

It is only in the last twenty years that radio astronomy has become one of the most important sciences. Yet in 1931 an American engineer, Karl Jansky, had already discovered the existence of radio waves. These waves come from the centre of our galaxy and are at least ten thousand times longer

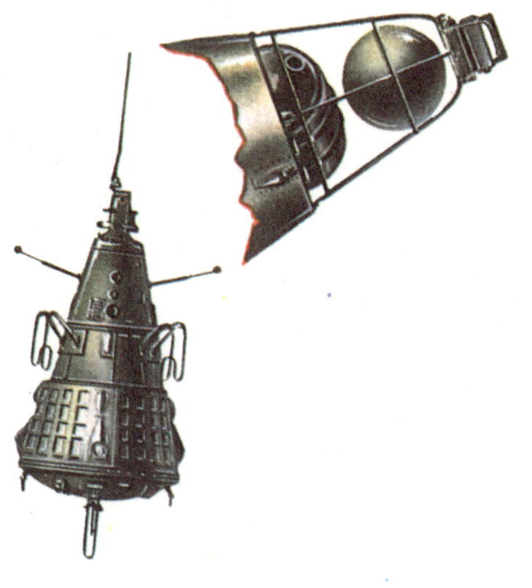

The Russian satellites *Sputnik II* (right) and *Sputnik III* (left)

than light waves.

To catch the very weak signals coming from outer space, enormous telescopes have had to be built to collect sufficient radiation for a signal to be detected. The telescope at Jodrell Bank is probably the most famous of these.

A special type of radio telescope is the radio interferometer. It detects the position of radio sources in the sky and shows the effects of interference of the radio waves coming from different directions.

When the first satellites were launched into space

It was 4 October 1957 when the Soviet Union launched Earth's first artificial satellite.

After this, a race began which brought an American triumph on 31 January 1958, when *Explorer I* discovered the famous Van Allen Belt. The discovery of this broad zone of radiation, named after the man who launched the instruments which found it, Dr. James Van Allen, had some far-reaching consequences. It made possible the design of equipment capable of shielding future astronauts from the danger of radiation.

Since that time many artificial satellites have been placed in orbit for military, scientific and communication purposes.

Man's landing on the Moon on 21 July 1969, owed much to these artificial satellites which orbit the Earth, revealing the secrets of space with their special instruments.

When the first microscopes appeared

The very small and the very large have always fascinated the human mind. Since the earliest times, men of science have tried to build instruments to investigate these two extremes.

For the infinitely small, or 'microcosm', as it is called in Greek, the microscope was invented, to magnify anything which cannot be seen with the naked eye.

The first microscopes appeared in the seventeenth century. They were extremely simple instruments, consisting of two fixed lenses in two sliding tubes. Magnifying and focusing were made possible by sliding one of the tubes inside the other.

Only opaque objects (objects which cannot be seen through) could be examined with these microscopes, however. It was not until the end of the seventeenth century that Campari, an Italian inventor, managed to overcome this difficulty by building a microscope for looking at transparent materials.

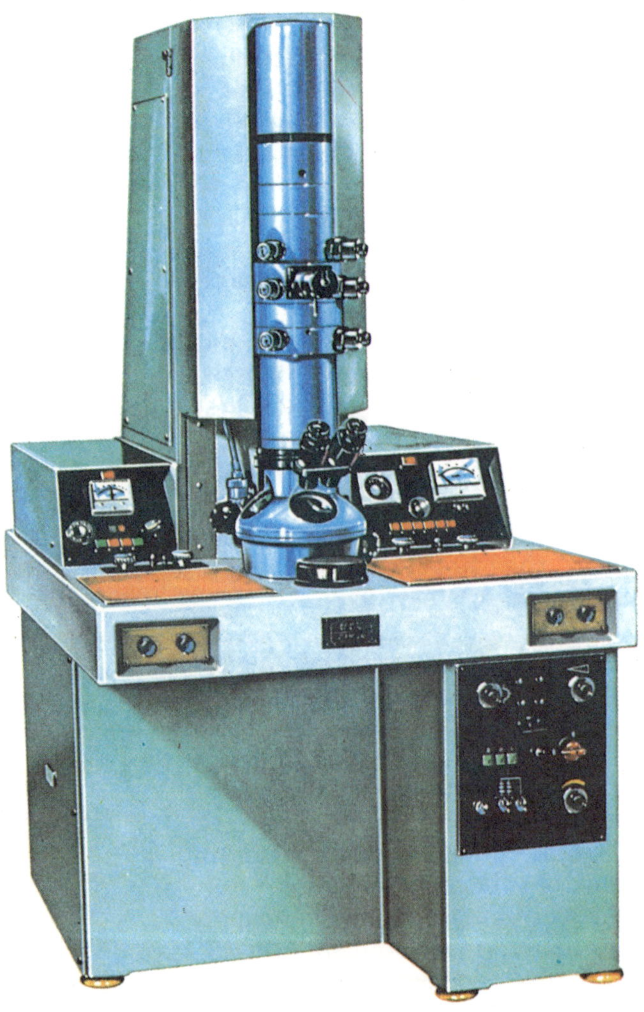

A modern electron microscope

When the compound microscope was invented

Human research never admits the word finished. This applies to all branches of science and is therefore also true of the world of microscopes.

The magnification achieved with the simple microscope was limited, and so the compound microscope with two principal lens systems was developed. In 1624, Galileo saw one of Cornelis Drebbel's instruments in Rome, and immediately introduced several improvements to it. He called his instrument a spyglass and made a present of it to some of his friends.

In this microscope the image enlarged by the first system is seen and enlarged again by the second system. Useful, that is clear, enlargements of up to 2,000 times are possible.

An instrument of this kind is of tremendous assistance in the study of certain bacteria and viruses, and the analyst is greatly helped by its magnifying power.

If new remedies are discovered for wiping out the many diseases which still threaten mankind, it will no doubt once again be thanks to the microscope, as it has been in the past.

When the use of the micro-scope spread

The microscope has been a useful instrument in all branches of science ever since it was invented. But it is only the rapid evolution of science and technology in the last twenty years that has brought about its wider use.

Work cannot even be carried on in some spheres of activity without the microscope.

In hospitals doctors use it to diagnose and then treat diseases; surgeons use it to perform delicate operations on complex and sensitive parts of the body such as the eye or the ear.

In the electronics industry the microscope permits high precision work which would otherwise be impossible.

Where the microscope is the most essential piece of equipment, however, is in research laboratories. The examination of botanical and animal cells takes place with the help of the microscope. It is also used in the sciences of petrology and metallurgy to obtain information on rocks and metals.

The microscope takes part in all kinds of complicated investigations, without which many stages in the progress of man would be lost.

When the electron microscope was invented

The first electron microscope was built by M. Knoll and E. Ruska in Berlin in 1932. Its development was rapid and in a few years its magnifying power had been increased from 17 to 400 times.

Its inventors despaired of the instrument ever working properly, as it was so difficult to keep the vacuum needed inside the optical column for all the electrons to multiply easily and produce an image.

In 1936, however, the electron microscope was at last demonstrated as an instrument of practical use.

Nowadays, electron microscopes have reached such a degree of perfection and are so useful that they can make enlargements of hundreds of thousands of times.

It was a French physicist, Louis de Broglie, who was the true father of the electron microscope. In fact, in 1924 he had managed to detect the wave-like nature of electrons, which behave like waves when fired in beams. It was therefore de Broglie who put forward the basic theory for what, some years later, became the electron microscope.

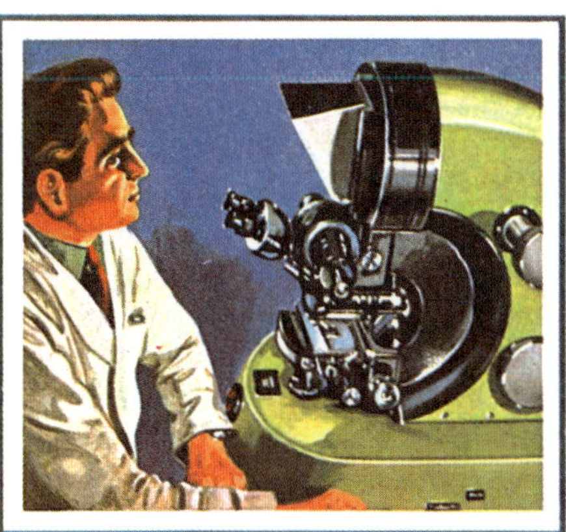

Phillips armoured dress of 1856

Galeazzi diving armour

When diving to the bottom of the sea was first considered

Although enormous progress in science and technology has unveiled many of nature's secrets, a world which is still largely unexplored and unknown is that of the bottom of the sea. The shape of the ocean bed, the behaviour of currents, the animal-life living in the depths, are still for the most part a mystery to us.

The vivid immagination of the writer Jules Verne (1828–1905), anticipates the age of underwater exploration in some of his adventure stories. His strange machines for exploring the bottom of the sea were much admired in his life-time and actually built by some confident enthusiasts.

Towards the middle of the nineteenth century, protective clothing and diving gear were made for the first deep-sea divers.

The development of this early apparatus was somewhat slow, partly because the divers' safety presented some serious problems as they were exposed to dangers of every kind.

When the first deep descent was made

The first attempts to break through the 'water barrier', that is to dive not tens of metres but hundreds of metres to the bottom of the sea, were made in the early 1930s. In 1934 an American naturalist, William Beebe, dived to 923 metres using a sphere tied to a support ship by strong steel cables.

Fifteen years later, in 1949, another American scientist, Otis Barton, dived to the exceptional depth of 1,360 metres, using the same method as Beebe.

These early explorers of the ocean bed were delighted with their discoveries. They were the first to see some of the sea's unknown marvels: strange-shaped fish, rocks encrusted with mysterious weeds and shells, darkness streaked with flashes of darting lights.

Beebe tells that he was so intent on looking at everything and remembering what he had seen that he did not realize he had been sitting on a monkey-wrench for hours.

When the first submarine was constructed

Diving suits, diving bells, air chambers, were all apparatus used for exploring the bottom of the sea but not for moving about in it.

It was the incomparable Leonardo da Vinci who had the first idea of a ship which could navigate both on and under the surface of the water.

In 1624 Cornelis Drebbel, a Dutch inventor, tried to make a submarine in England. He successfully manoeuvred the craft in the river Thames at depths of from 4 to 5 metres beneath the surface. On one occasion King James I is said to have gone aboard.

150 years later, in 1774, another inventor, Day, lost his life in a vessel intended to remain underwater for 12 hours in Plymouth Sound.

The earliest recorded submarine to be employed as an offensive weapon was made in 1776 by the American marine engineer, David Bushnell. A one-man submarine built of wood in the shape of a pear, it attempted to sink a British man-of-war in New York harbour during the American War of Independence.

The next attempt was made towards the end of the eighteenth century when another American, Robert Fulton, demonstrated a submarine to the French authorities, remaining 4 hours underwater at a depth of 8 metres.

The basic idea of these early engineers was to increase the weight of the hull until it was so heavy that it sank because it was stronger than the upward pressure of the water which had kept it afloat. The weight was provided by enormous quantities of water let into suitably positioned ballast tanks. To resurface, the water was pumped out again. This system is based on Archimedes' well-known principle and is still applied to modern submarines.

When Piccard set up his records

The Swiss scientist Auguste Piccard was a man born for adventure. After travelling through the sky in a balloon, in 1938 he turned to the problems of underwater exploration.

Piccard's invention has a special name: the bathyscaphe. It consists of a bouyancy chamber for floating the vehicle and of a spherical observation cabin.

The great advantage of the bathyscaphe is that it can move about on its own, without having to be linked to a support ship. In this way it is similar to a submarine but it can go down to far greater depths.

The bathyscaphe has made some exciting achievements in its short life.

In 1953 Piccard, with his son Jacques, beat all previous records for deep-sea diving. Using the bathyscaphe *Trieste*, named after the Italian city because it had been built almost entirely in Italy, the two brave scientists descended to a depth of 3,150 metres in the waters of the Gulf of Naples, off the island of Ponza.

In 1958, the *Trieste* was acquired by the U.S. Navy and was equipped with a new cabin. Under the Navy's auspices, on 7 January 1960, Jacques Piccard dived to 7,025 metres near the Marina Islands, in the West Pacific.

A few days later, on 23 January, Jacques, accompanied by Don Walsh of the U.S. Navy, reached 10,916 metres in the Marina Trench, the deepest sea trench in the world.

The first submarines were based on the famous principle of Archimedes

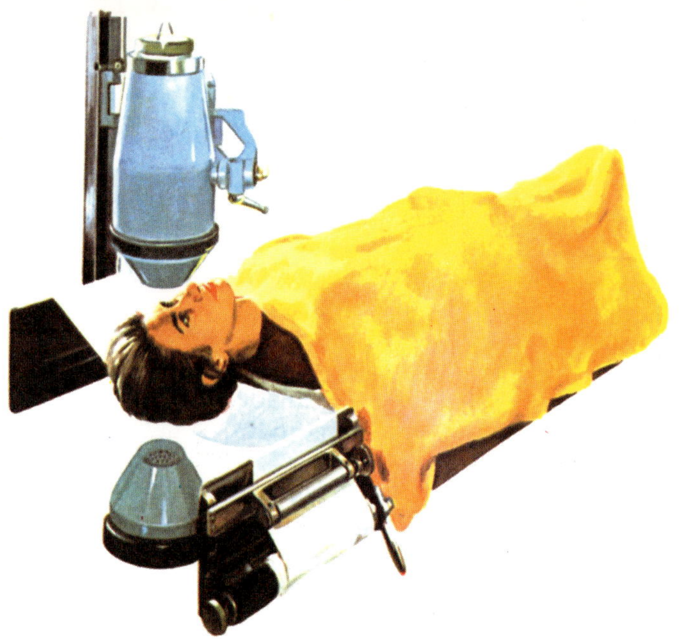

When X-rays were discovered

In 1803 John Dalton put forward his theory that matter is made up of indivisible particles called atoms, and another ninety-two years passed before the German physicist, Wilhelm Conrad Röntgen, discovered X-rays.

The contribution X-rays have made and are still making to many branches of the biological and physical sciences, is a measure of the importance of this discovery. With X-rays it has been possible to build a super-microscope which can not only see atoms but can also see inside them. Röntgen's discovery, in fact, was the start of modern atomic and molecular physics, which is the study of the structure of matter and its constituents.

Although X-rays have so many uses, they are best-known in the field of medicine. They help diagnose the early stages of diseases and then assist in the treatment of them by killing cancerous cells in biological structures or stopping the cells from splitting up and spreading. They are of invaluable use in hospitals today.

When radioactivity was discovered

Radioactivity was discovered by the French physicist, Henri Becquerel. In 1896 he was examining uranium salts when he noticed that they emitted radioactive rays. Then in 1898 Pierre and Marie Curie succeeded in separating radium. This gives off rays so powerful that they can penetrate solid surfaces.

The first nuclear reactor was built in the United States in 1942. The first experimental nuclear bomb exploded in New Mexico in 1945.

When the peaceful uses of atomic energy began

The military use of nuclear power calls to mind the horror of Hiroshima and Nagasaki. But nuclear power also has a great potential for good which can be used when its force is released.

The atomic age began on 2 December 1942, when Enrico Fermi made the first controlled nuclear chain reaction. It already has many peaceful applications to its credit.

In 1956 the first nuclear power station in the world was opened at Calder Hall, in Cumberland, to produce electricity commercially.

On 10 December 1967, a tremendous explosion was set off 1,300 metres under the ground in New Mexico. New ways of using nuclear explosives for peaceful purposes were being tested.

In 1957 the International Atomic Energy Agency was created under the auspices of the United Nations. The aim of the I.A.E.A. is to ensure that nuclear energy is used for peace to finance research projects for peaceful purposes.

When the first atomic submarine was built

The appearance of the first nuclear-propelled submarine in the history of navigation dates back to January 1955. The *Nautilus,* named in memory of Jules Verne's famous imaginary submarine, could sail twice round the world using only 4 kilos of Uranium 235.

But perhaps the most spectacular adventure of this American submarine was its voyage under the ice-cap of the North Pole in 1958, a feat which met with complete success.

Following the successful trials with the *Nautilus,* the U.S. navy embarked on an extensive building programme of nuclear-powered submarines of several different types.

When the first rails were used

English miners were the first people to think of tracks for guiding the wheels of their coal wagons.

The idea probably came to them from the furrows made by the continual trundling of the wagons through the underground tunnels.

The furrows were eventually edged with wooden lines, kept apart by sleepers, also of wood. As they wore down, the lines were repaired with iron face-plates but these did considerable damage to the wagon wheels so that, in time, they too had to be made of iron.

The first 'railroads' were built in England for horse-drawn coaches.

Finally, in 1797, the first real rails were made. They were cast iron rods, 90 centimetres long and weighing 22 kilos each, produced at the Coalbrook Dale

foundry by Richard Reynolds.

The first vehicles to travel on rails were pulled by animals or men.

Even after the steam engine had been invented, animal traction continued for many years.

For example, the first public railway was operated by the Surrey Iron Railway Company which had been created through an Act of Parliament passed in 1801. The railway was opened in 1803 and ran between Wandsworth and Croydon, drawn by horses.

Trevithick's *Catch-Me-Who-Can*

When the steam engine replaced the horse

On 21 February 1804 the first self-propelled locomotive, built by Richard Trevithick, was demonstrated in Penydaren, Glamorgan.

When perfected, the engine managed to pull up to five wagons with a load of 10 tons of goods and seventy passengers. Running along at speeds of up to 8 kilometres an hour over a distance of 16 kilometres, it seemed to many people a wonder hardly to be surpassed.

There were many others who did not like the new machine, however, and who were convinced it would not work. They insisted that as the rails and the wheels rubbed against each other they would create such friction that it would stop the train. So Trevithick organized a kind of train circus as a publicity stunt, calling his locomotive *Catch-Me-Who-Can*. He chose a site near London's Euston Road and, at 24 kilometres an hour, his little train chugged round and round to the enthusiasm of the assembled crowd.

When Stephenson built his *Rocket*

Trevithick is generally regarded as the father of the steam train but the most famous figure of the pioneer days of railways is George Stephenson who was born in Newcastle upon Tyne in 1781.

An enginewright and mechanic at the Killingworth colliery in Northumberland, he managed to find the money to build a locomotive which he called *My Lord* and which was successfully tested on the tramroads of the colliery in 1814.

Various kinds of locomotive were designed by Stephenson and they were all remarkably successful.

The young engineer became so enthusiastic about the new means of locomotion that he decided to launch himself into the exciting task of providing steam engines for public railways.

In 1822 Stephenson was appointed engineer of the Stockton and Darlington Railway. On 27 September 1825 the first steam passenger service in railway history was inaugurated. Speeds of up to 24 kilometres an hour were reached.

Conclusive proof of the efficiency of Stephenson's steam engines came on 6 October 1829.

Five locomotives entered for trials set by the directors of the Liverpool and Manchester Railway but only Stephenson's *Rocket* passed and so won the competition and a prize of £500.

It travelled at up to 39 kilometres per hour, fully laden.

On 15 September 1830 the railway age began. That day the Liverpool to Manchester line was opened, the first to be operated entirely by steam.

When steam replaced sails

The nineteenth century is also known as the steam age, which reflects what an important part steam played in every sphere of life.

At the same time as the steam train was making its trial runs, the American, Robert Fulton, was designing and testing his first river boat propelled not by the force of the wind but by two big wheels worked by a steam engine.

His steamboat, as Fulton called it, made its maiden voyage on 9 August 1807 and, eight days later, it started a 240-kilometre trip up the Hudson River, from New York to Albany. It took 32 hours to accomplish this journey, a speed which was soon considerably increased.

In the war of 1812–14 against Great Britain, Fulton built the first steam warship.

The new ships were so successful that they soon began to supplant sailing ships, despite the fierce struggle which the owners of the sailing ships put up against the 'dangerous' new invention.

In May and June 1819 the first ocean-going steam ship, the *Savannah*, crossed the Atlantic from the United States to Ireland.

The voyage cannot be said to have been a complete success, however, as the engines only took over from the sails for 85 hours because supplies of coal ran out.

The early steam ships still depended partly on sails for auxiliary power. It was a long fight between sail and steam, and at the beginning of the twentieth century there were still plenty of sailing ships plying the oceans. But they were now economic only for transporting non-perishable food-stuffs over long distances.

Stephenson's *Rocket*

When iron was first used in shipbuilding

Up until the 1840s the vast majority of ships were made entirely of wood. There were very few iron bits and those were non-essential. Although the hull had changed shape, it differed little in construction from the way ship-builders had worked for thousands of years.

The first important composite ship, that is one constructed of wood and iron or steel, was the *Great Britain*, built at Bristol in 1845. It proved its strength and endurance when, in 1846, it ran aground in Dundrum Bay in Ireland. Although it remained aground for eleven months, it was then refloated and continued in existence until 1937.

News of the system spread far and wide because it marked an important advance in shipbuilding. It combined the flexibility of wooden planking with the strength of an iron framework. The iron's main advantage, its solidity, was happily married with wood's best feature, its flexibility.

The greatest obstacle to be

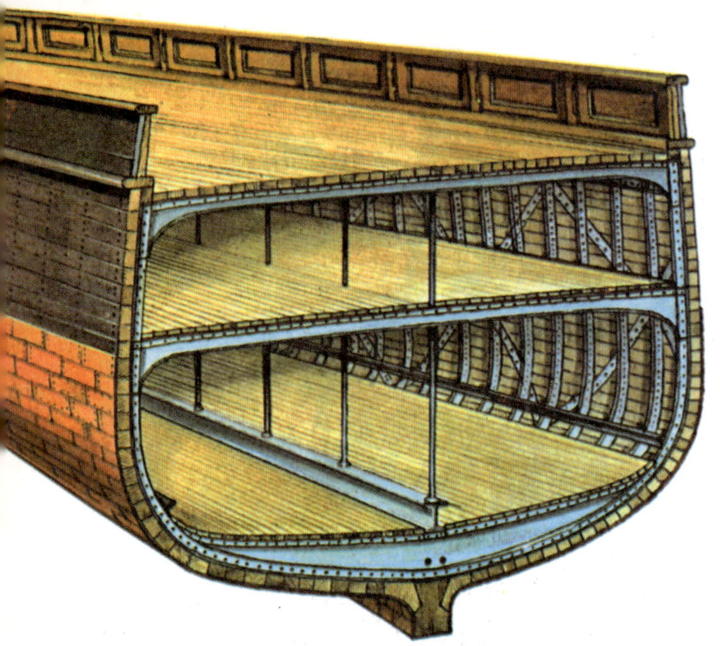

Composite ship (made of wood and metal)

overcome was the galvanic action which the sea water set up between wood and metal, causing them to rot.

It is a well-known fact that contact between two heterogeneous bodies (bodies of a different kind) produces electric currents which may be very destructive.

In the case of ships the trouble was accentuated by the presence of salt water.

The remedy was found by insulating the points of contact between wood and iron with rubber. This type of mixed construction was used for about twenty years, particularly in the cargo-carrying clippers.

Towards the middle of the nineteenth century, the first giants of the ocean were built for long, fast voyages. One of the most famous was the *Great Eastern*, launched in 1858, and one of the strongest ships ever built. It was the first ocean liner, with a crew of 400 and able to carry 4,000 passengers.

When the first motor cars appeared

The first automobile, or self-propelled vehicle, in history was invented in 1769 by Nicolas Cugnot, a French military engineer. It was a kind of tricycle with a strong frame on which a two-cylinder steam engine rested. It could pull a load of 5 tons at a speed of 5 kilometres an hour.

This ancestor of the motor car is now to be seen in Paris but looks more frightening than exciting to ride on.

By 1862 steam engine exhibitions were being organized. The bulky machines looked no different from the ones which ran on rails.

Among the few successes at the first exhibitions were the machines of Amédée Bollée, who was determined to make a 'practical horseless carriage'. In 1873 his first vehicle was ready. He called it *Obéissant*, the French word for obedient, because it was so easy to steer. It was a kind of bus with steering-gear on its two front wheels. The success of the *Obéssiant* was so encouraging that Bollée continued his series of 'automobile' machines.

An important event in the progress of road transport was the discovery of the internal combustion engine.

Following this, in 1876, the German, Nikolaus August Otto, patented a kind of four-stroke engine based on a design by the Frenchman, Beau de Rochas.

But it was not until 1882 that Gottlieb Daimler, another German, built the first light engines. Three years later, Daimler's son drove 3 kilometres with one of these engines installed in a four-wheeled carriage.

Another motoring pioneer was

the German, Karl Friedrich Benz. In 1885 he built a car which was to prove highly successful.

French manufacturers were the first to realize the importance of these inventions. Using the patents of Daimler and Benz, they laid the foundations of the huge industry which is still flourishing today and has known such names as Panhard, Levassor and Peugeot.

The first Motor Show was held in Paris in 1887.

When the first underground railway was built

In 1863 London must have already been having its traffic problems because that was the year when the first underground railway system in the world was opened. It had been specially designed to reduce the city's traffic, which had become too congested and noisy.

It was a steam railway which soon became very popular with Londoners who made regular use of it. The line was about four and a half kilometres long and linked the stations of Paddington, Euston, King's Cross and Farringdon Street.

The trains were quite comfortable and travelled at remarkable speeds for those days. They could carry 27,000 passengers a day.

This first underground railway was extended to form an inner circle in 1884.

In 1890 the 'tube' was built by boring through the earth from underground working sites. It was the City and South London Railway and ran from the City to Stockwell. For the first time an electrified line was used which set going small electric locomotives.

It was the forerunner of the modern high-speed underground.

Yarrow and Hilditch's motor car

Obéissant, **1873**

Hewetson's Benz *Victoria,* 1895

137

When the rack railway was invented

It is very difficult for smooth steel wheels to grip smooth steel rails. This soon became one of the disadvantages of railways. Even today, the steepest slope which train wheels dare attempt has a gradient of only one metre in every eleven.

Several people tried to overcome this problem. In 1812 the Englishman, John Blenkinsop, invented an engine with special toothed wheels which engaged with a rail, also toothed, fitted to the track.

The rack railway is still widely used for short distances in hilly areas. It passes through mountainous regions such as the Alps and goes to the summit of Snowdon in North Wales, and Mount Washington and Pike's Peak in the United States.

A special kind of railway is the funicular, or cable-railway, in which trains are pulled by metal cables. These railways are used in mountainous countries, such as Switzerland, to transport skiers and tourists.

When the first monorail was built

It is widely believed that the monorail is a recent achievement. Yet the first design was patented in 1821 and built in 1824.

A German monorail which has been operating regularly since 1901 is the famous *Schwebebahn*, which means 'suspension-railway', and runs on an overhead rail from Wuppertal Barmen to Wuppertal Vohwinkel.

The Alweg monorail system was tested in Germany in 1952 on the Cologne-Fuhbingen line. This is a track system except that only one rail is used, the carriages travelling over a concrete beam.

Another monorail system, called Safage, was tested in Texas in 1956. The cars are suspended from trolleys with rubber-tyred wheels driven by diesel motors.

In the 1960s supporters of the monorail claimed it as the answer to large-city transport problems. However, monorail systems have now been superseded by maglev trains, which travel by magnetic force along tracks built at ground level or above the ground.

Alweg-type six-car monorail train in Japan

When the first automatic railway was opened

In 1927 the first train to operate without a driver or guard went into service in Britain. It has continued to carry London's mail ever since. Its wagons have now covered more than 80 million kilometres. A similar completely automatic mail train is operating in Brussels.

A very recent invention is a kind of vehicle which has almost no friction, or resistance to motion, because it does not rub along the ground. It is the maglev train, which uses magnetic levitation to float a short distance above its track. Powerful permanent magnets and electromagnets in the train and along the track produce the force that lifts the train. The train also has a linear induction motor, a kind of electric motor that produces magnetic force to move the train along the track.

When the Montgolfier was invented

It proved so difficult to beat the force of gravity, that many inventors turned their attention to machines which would fly by using gases lighter than air.

The problem was eventually solved by the Montgolfier brothers, the sons of a French paper merchant. Employed by their father in his business, they had learned about the different kinds of paper. Their enthusiasm for science did the rest: on 4 June 1783, at Annonay, a village near Lyons, the first balloon in history rose into the sky and became known as the Montgolfier, after its inventors.

The two brothers had worked from a simple theory which proved to be correct: if hot air rises, it must only need to be sealed in a light-weight envelope for the envelope to be pushed upwards, too. The hot air was produced by burning straw and wool in a brazier slung beneath the balloon.

When the first people rose into the air

The first people to rise into the air were the French pioneers Pilâtre de Rozier and the Marquis d'Arlandes. On 21 November 1783 at Paris, they made an historic flight of 9 kilometres that lasted 25 minutes, ascending in a hot-air balloon that was built by the Montgolfier brothers. The men returned safely to the ground. If we remember that those early balloons were something completely new and that the first balloonists were faced with

Montmartre funicular railway up the hill to the Sacré Coeur

The balloon of Pilâtre de Rozier and the Marquis d'Arlandes (left)

Giffard's dirigible

Napoleon wanted to use balloons to invade England (left)

innumerable dangers, their achievement seems even more staggering.

Pilâtre de Rozier's flight attracted so much attention that the Montgolfier brothers were encouraged to continue their experiments. The daring French physicist who was the first to venture into the sky may be regarded as the forerunner of the modern astronauts.

When the first cross-Channel balloon flight was made

Two weeks after the first balloon flight, another ascent was made by the French physicist Jacques Charles and an assistant named Robert. Their balloon contained the light gas hydrogen instead of hot air, and this flight covered 43 kilometres.

These achievements sparked off a craze for ballooning and it became a popular sport. Pioneers vied to perform the most daring flights, though were often frustrated by the wind, which could stop or even veer to take the balloonists in another direction. Then the main goal of the pioneers became the English Channel.

On 7 January 1785 Blanchard and Jeffries crossed the Channel, a highly difficult and dangerous feat. The following June de Rozier and a friend were killed during their attempt to repeat this achievement and fly from France to England.

When airships were invented

Every day it became increasingly apparent that balloons could not rely on unpredictable air currents but would have to be made more manageable, with an engine and a rudder to steer them.

In 1852, again in France, the first airship was launched. It had been made by Henri Giffard who had risen from being an ordinary railway worker to becoming an excellent engineer. He called his invention *Giffard I*.

Steerable airships, or dirigibles as they were known, made some memorable achievements. They took a major step forward in 1872

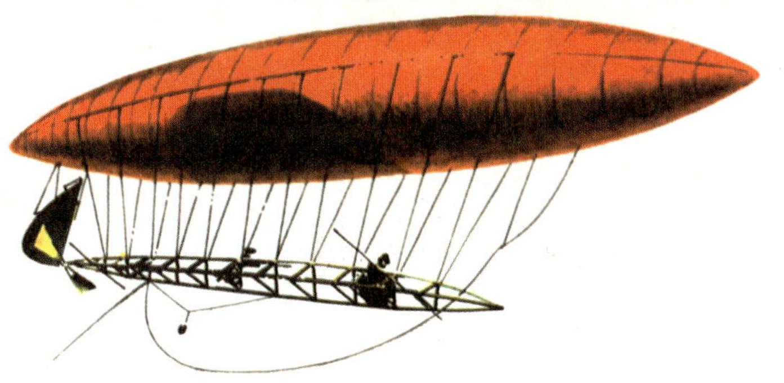

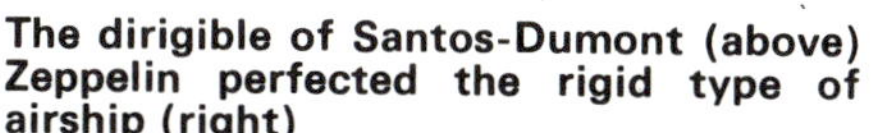

The dirigible of Santos-Dumont (above) Zeppelin perfected the rigid type of airship (right)

when their steam engines were replaced by internal combustion engines. This innovation was the work of a German engineer, Paul Haenlein.

The two main features of the dirigibles were their rigid envelope and their engine. They soon became so easy to handle that they were used commercially for carrying goods.

Steerable airships flourished over a period of 85 years, from 24 September 1852 (the *Giffard I* at Paris) to 6 May 1937 (the *Zeppelin LZ 129* at Lakehurst, U.S.A.).

The most famous airships of all were the Zeppelins. They appeared on the flying scene in 1900, when the German officer, Graf Ferdinand von Zeppelin, flew over Lake Constance in an 126-metre-long airship which he named after himself.

Another Zeppelin closed the history of the airships when it burst into flames in the sky over Lakehurst on 6 May 1937. Thirty-six people lost their lives in the fierce explosion.

When 'heavier-than-air' machines beat the 'lighter-than-air'

Leonardo da Vinci's flying machine was built so that the pilot moved the wings with his hands and feet, and the tail with his head.

Leonardo had designed machines for flying but, apart from their curiosity value, his plans did not produce any concrete results.

For over three centuries, brave and sometimes fanatical men continued to make attempts to fly.

This is the period which spans Leonardo's inventions and the first serious efforts made by modern technology to break through the barrier of the pull of the Earth's gravity.

One of the best remembered is William Henson's aerial steam carriage. This was designed in about 1850 and owed much to the work of Sir George Cayley who had made a model glider in 1804 and later built a full-sized glider.

By the time airships had reached their peak, the aeroplane was born. Clément Ader and Otto

Leonardo's helicopter

When the first aeroplanes were invented

In the field of aeronautics, each step forward brought the conquest of the air that much nearer attainment.

As ballooning had had two brothers, the Montgolfiers, so mechanical flight had as its originators another two brothers, the Americans Wilbur and Orville Wright of Dayton, Ohio. Their machine was a biplane, or an aeroplane with two pairs of wings, similar to Lilienthal's glider but powered by a 16 horse-power internal combustion engine and weighing about 62 kilos.

On the morning of 17 December 1903, the Wright brothers made their first flight in this machine. It took place near the Kill Devil Hills, Kitty Hawk, North Carolina.

The flight only lasted 12 seconds but, at a later attempt, they travelled more than 500 metres. Many people think of 17 December 1903 as the true date of the start of modern aviation.

Wilbur Wright went to France and first flew in public near Le Mans in August 1908. By the end of the year he had made over one hundred flights in Europe, had broken every record and had even made a flight lasting two hours and twenty minutes.

On 25 July 1909 Louis Blériot, flying a machine powered by an engine designed by the Italian, Alessandro Anzani, crossed the Channel from Calais to Dover.

On 7 January 1910 Hubert Latham climbed to a height of more than 1,600 metres.

Again in 1910, on 23 September, Geo Chavez, a Peruvian living in Paris, crossed the Alps on a tragic flight which cost him his life, just as his journey was ended.

Lilienthal are generally accepted as the founders of aviation.

In 1890 Ader succeeded in lifting his propeller machine a few centimetres off the ground and making it fly for 50 metres: this was the first real human flight.

Lilienthal, on the other hand, decided against a steam engine like Ader's in favour of the wind and natural air currents. He de-

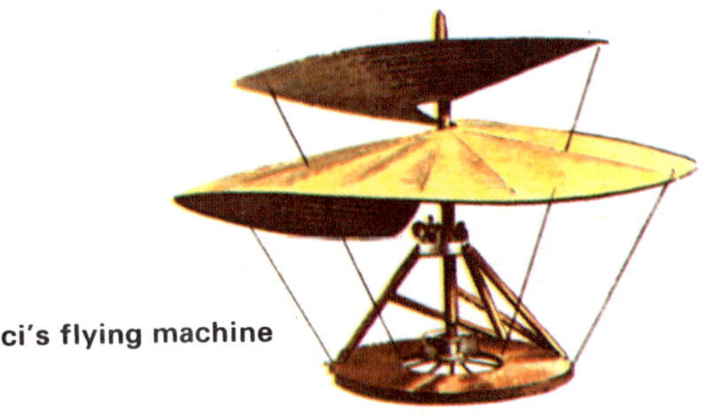

Leonardo da Vinci's flying machine

signed a kind of glider with fixed wings which was meant to slide off the top of a hill.

Lilienthal's experiments continued successfully for a number of years, and as a result of his studies aeronautics became an exact science.

Lilienthal experimented himself with his gliders and it was on one of the flights that he crashed and was killed in 1896.

At the time of this fatal accident he had already made about a hundred launchings.

Henson's Aerial Steam Carriage, 1842

When aeroplanes were first used in war

In the ten years following the Wright brothers' flight, aeronautical conquests went from strength to strength.

On 29 September 1913 the Frenchman, Maurice Prévost, succeeded in reaching 200 kilometres an hour in a French-made monoplane. It was an amazing record which heralded even greater and more spectacular progress within a short space of time.

For the First World War then broke out and to many it seemed that the aeroplane must become a first-rate war machine.

Manoeuvrable, high-speed aeroplanes were quickly built, more for reconnaissance flights than for actual combat.

The Italians, who had already experimented with aeroplanes in action in the Libyan war of 1911, were also the first to use them in the new conflict.

By the end of the war there was an active aircraft industry in several European countries.

Great progress had also been made in training pilots, who had had a wonderful opportunity to gain experience on active service.

In the field of civil aviation, aeroplanes were used from 1914 both for carrying passengers (in Florida) and mail (in Italy). Their use as a civil transport grew steadily from 1919. Scheduled routes were established in Europe and in local regions throughout the world, and special designs of airliner came into service.

The seaplane, which could take off and land on water, had been invented in 1911 in the United States. It, too, was greatly improved during the war years.

Wright's glider in flight

When the first transatlantic flight was made

In 1919 the first Atlantic crossing was made from Newfoundland to Ireland by the Englishmen, Alcock and Brown.

In 1926 Commander Richard Byrd of the United States Navy became the first person to fly over the North Pole.

1927 brought the most famous of the flying achievements when Lindbergh crossed the vast expanse of the Atlantic Ocean in a solo, non-stop flight from New York to Paris.

In 1930–31 a squadron of Italian seaplanes flew from Orbetello in Italy to Rio de Janeiro in Brazil.

In 1938, on the eve of the Second World War, the Italian, Pezzi, set up his altitude record of 17,083 metres, a record which has still not been beaten by a piston-engined plane.

The wind tunnel where the Wright brothers experimented with different kinds of wing

Engine built for a 1909 aeroplane

Orville Wright's first historic flight on 17 December 1903

A Westland Whirlwind saves a shipwreck survivor on a rubber dinghy (left)
Soldiers dropping from a Mil Mi-4 on to a Russian submarine (right)

A Sikorsky S-61 Ns (above)
The huge Mil Mi-10 has a platform big enough for a bus (below)

When jet planes were invented

Although research into the construction of jet engines had begun earlier it was not until 1936 that Frank Whittle received support for his ideas on jet propulsion. His first successful engine was built in the following year. During the Second World War a few high performance jet machines were tested, but they were seldom used for military purposes.

After the war, civil aviation turned to jet propulsion but it was a slow process as it usually took seven years of lengthy experiments and research from the design stage to operational maturity.

The change from propeller-driven to jet aeroplanes began with the introduction into service of the de Havilland Comet by British Overseas Airways Corporation in 1952. During the late 1950s, the French-built Caravelles, powered by two Rolls Royce turbojet engines, were widely used by European and American airlines.

Today the volume of air traffic means that bigger and bigger machines are needed, both for freight and passenger services. One of the best known is the Jumbo Jet which can carry 490 passengers at a time.

From the point of view of speed, too, the new planes are beating all the most optimistic forecasts.

The Anglo-French Concorde can carry passengers at 2,300 kilometres an hour, more than twice the speed of sound.

Military aircraft have already been flying at three times the speed of sound for over ten years.

The day when it will take less than 120 minutes to cross the Atlantic is not far off.

When the first helicopters were built

To find the origins of the helicopter we have to go back to the helicopter toys of the ancient Chinese, and to Leonardo da Vinci who, in about 1500, designed a spiral wing which was meant to take off by rotating in the air. This design, of which a model was apparently made, was not known until late in the nineteenth century.

In 1784 the Frenchmen, Launoy and Bienvenu, designed the first successful model helicopter in Europe and presented it to the Academy of Sciences.

During the nineteenth century many models were invented that were operated by steam or twisted rubber, some of them making successful flights.

In 1907 the first helicopter able to carry a man was built by Paul Cornu and made a brief vertical flight. Later in the same year Louis Bréguet constructed a helicopter which rose one and a half metres off the ground for about a minute.

Between 1915 and 1928 numerous attempts were made to build a working helicopter. The first successful and practical helicopter was the Focke-Achgelis of 1937 but it was not until 1939 that the Russian born Igor Sikorsky designed and flew the first really practical machine in the U.S.A. In 1941 he broke all previous records by remaining in the air for 92 minutes. Most modern helicopters derive from his work.

Helicopters can fly up and down, forwards, backwards or sideways. They are perfect for vertical flight and are used for an increasing variety of jobs, both military and civilian.

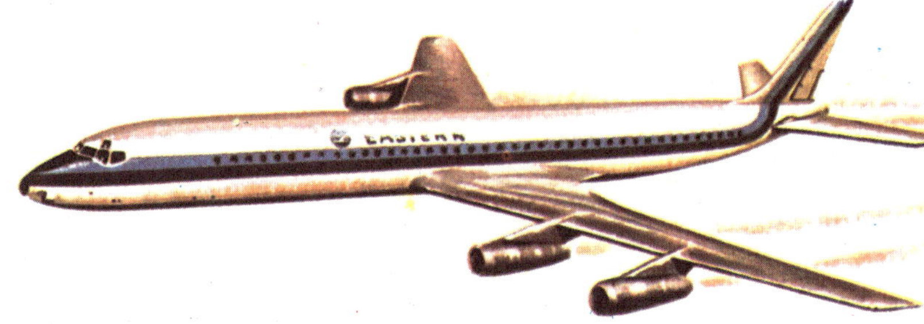

The DC-8 Super 61

Concorde landing with its nose down to give the pilot better visibility

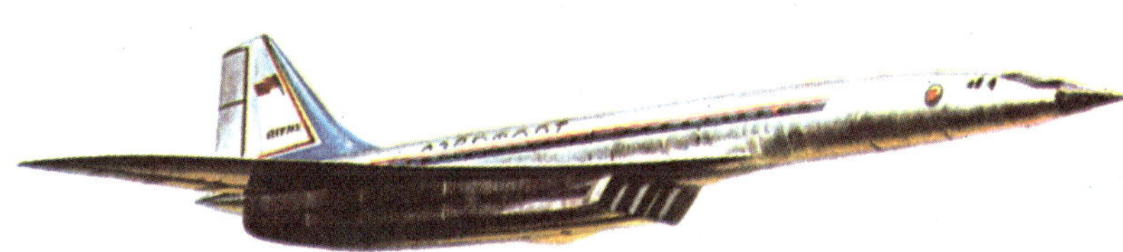

The Russian Tu-144, the first supersonic civilian aircraft

The Boeing 747, the first Jumbo

When the first photograph was taken

Although the invention of photography is comparatively recent, the camera obscura, which is the darkened box with a hole in one wall which forms the essential part of a camera, has been known since about the year A.D. 1000.

Documents of that period record that an Arab, Alhazen, had described the principle of the camera obscura.

It was not until 1812, however, that the first lens for taking photographs was made. It was a concave-convex system (curved inward on one side and outward on the other) and was invented by the English chemist, William Hyde Wollaston.

This invention led to the start of photography, which was the work of another chemist, the Frenchman Joseph Nicéphore Niepce. He succeeded in fixing the image transmitted by the camera obscura on a sensitive metal plate.

Compared with the rapid ex-posure times of modern cameras, the eight hours it took Niepce to expose his first picture seem an eternity, yet this was the true beginning of the history of photography.

The camera was invented by Louis Daguerre, who in 1829 formed a partnership with Niepce. In 1839 Daguerre succeeded in putting together a camera with a lens. The photographs taken with this first camera were called 'daguerreotypes', after their inventor.

When photographic film was introduced in 1875, replacing the heavy plates of the daguerreotypes, modern cameras came into being.

When the cinema began

Photography was well advanced when the cinema began.

Attempts to animate pictures date back to the magic lantern, but it was not until the end of the nineteenth century that the cinema arrived.

The Americans, Germans, English and French had all been racing against each other to be the first to produce a 'movie'.

Victory went to two brothers, Louis and Auguste Lumière, who projected their first film to the public in a Paris hotel. It was 28 December 1895 and in a short while the news of the Lumière brothers' invention had spread all over the world.

At that time few people realized that a new art-form had been born. The majority thought of the motion picture as a piece of technical gadgetry intended for the few. But it soon became the most popular form of public entertainment.

The cinema was born silent, the actions generally being explained

by captions. In the most up-to-date cinema halls all that could be expected was a pianist paid to accompany the events on the screen with appropriate background music.

In October 1927 Al Jolson appeared in *The Jazz Singer*, a silent film with four talking or singing interludes. This was the start of sound in films.

All-talking pictures followed in 1928 with the film *The Lights of New York*.

Colour films, wide-screen presentations and stereophonic sound are now standard features that greatly enhance cinema entertainment.

When television began

The electronic system of television that we use today was developed in the United States in the 1920s and 1930s. It was preceded by a mechanical system that did not give high quality. By the outbreak of the Second World War in 1939 television was being broadcast in England, Germany and the United States.

It was not until 1950, however, after the war had finished, that the industry began to function efficiently again and in 1953 there were regular television programmes in many countries.

By 1960, programmes could be viewed for most of the afternoon and evening.

Although experiments in colour television have been carried on since the early days of television, regular colour broadcasting has only become widespread in the last twenty years.

During the same period, communications satellites have been developed to relay television programmes around the world.

When the transistor was invented

In 1918 a thermionic valve, which was an electronic valve in early radios, was as big as a milk bottle. This shows how important it was to the development of modern technology when the size of these instruments was gradually reduced.

By 1935 valves had been made much smaller and measured about 10 centimetres over all; during the Second World War this measurement was halved and in December 1947 the transistor was invented by John Bardeen, Walter Brattain and William Shockley.

The transistor is the component which replaces the cumbersome old valves. It amplifies electric currents and voltages so much that it can make enormous savings on size, weight and, above all, power consumption.

The industries which are completely transistorized today are portable radios, ballistic missiles and military equipment in general, various kinds of control systems, electronic computers and television.

When the first calculating machines were made

Some people have always disliked doing sums and have wanted calculating machines to do the work for them. The first calculating device was the abacus, widely used from ancient times.

The first 'multiplier' was invented in 1617 by the Scotsman, John Napier, the man who devised logarithms.

A few years later, in 1642, Blaise Pascal, the famous French philosopher and mathematician, invented an adding machine. It was worked by cog-wheels and could add up six-figure numbers by automatically moving the tens.

Gottfried Wilhelm Leibniz, another philosopher, then improved Pascal's machine to such an extent that it could even work out square roots.

Pascal was the first person to invent an instrument for adding up six-figure numbers by automatically moving the tens

When the computer age began

Between 1834–54 Charles Babbage designed and partly built an 'analytic engine' which may be said to be the first mechanical computer in history. It contained all the essential features on which modern computers are based. Development of this invention was hindered through lack of funds.

After many years, 'relays' were eventually produced. They are electromechanical devices which permit calculations to be made a thousand times faster than Babbage's machine.

A crucial step was taken with the discovery of valves which can speed up calculating even more. The invention of transistors in 1947 led to the modern machines which can operate thousands of millions of times faster than Babbage's.

When electronic computers were first used

Since the 1940s a new word has come into our vocabularies. It is the word 'computers' and refers to the complicated calculating machines which can even plan and check much of what is being tried out in science and technology.

Computers are also often called electronic programmers or electronic brains. Early uses of computers at universities were for scientific and engineering calculations, but in modern life the functions they perform are becoming more and more intricate and varied.

Apart from replacing hundreds of specialists who were once required to work out complicated calculations, they can help in programming the lessons in several schools at once from television terminals; they can give banks a minute-by-minute account of the monetary situation, make a catalogue of the books in a library, make public opinion surveys and even compose electronic music.

It is a fact that the scientific and technological progress of tomorrow is wholly dependent on these amazing machines which can perform millions of calculations in a second.

Computers are generally operated by using a keyboard to feed instructions and information into the computer or with simple hand controls. However, new computers which will respond to commands given by the human voice are already in an advanced state of development.

It will then be possible for them to leave the world of the specialist and enter into the daily lives of us all.

When the computer made the space age possible

The space age has also come about through the introduction of computers. These incredible machines have been able to make calculations which would have taken experts thousands of hours of work, with a strong possibility of mistakes by the end of it.

Computers, on the other hand, can perform complex calculations in a fraction of a second with total accuracy.

Continual checks on all the flying equipment are essential for space travel. Without computers this task would be impossible.

The American Apollo project in the sixties used a computer with the most massive information retrieval system in existence. It operates 125 separate programs.

The 'count-down' which we all know from watching space launches on television, is made possible by computers. They carry out a second-by-second check of all the rocket's equipment from its final preparation to the actual take-off.

The launch of the space shuttle is controlled by several computers that also check each other's performance. All must agree for the launch to proceed.

WHEN THE PLANTS IN OUR LIVES BEGAN

The first men on Earth did not know how to grow plants or breed animals. To get food they spent the day hunting or gathering fruit and seeds which ripened naturally in the woods. In the summer life was easy: game was plentiful and the trees and bushes provided fruit and berries of every kind. But when the snow came the animals hid and the plants were bare and no longer gave fruit.

Even if the women of the tribe had saved food for the winter, it was very difficult for them to preserve it. In time the fruit withered and supplies of meat ran out.

It was then that man discovered that there were other plants which could save him from starving. They were woodland plants with dry fruits which did not wither in the winter: the hazel trees, chestnuts, oaks and walnuts.

In many lake-settlements large quantities of shells and other traces of these fruits have been found, a clear sign that they were an important food for primitive man. The fruit of the dogwood, or cornel tree, another common woodland plant, was also highly prized in prehistoric times, when primitive man had to gather the fruits of the woods because he did not know how to farm.

In the pile-dwellings of Lake Ledro, in northern Italy, incredible amounts of dogwood berry stones have been found, buried in the mud at the bottom of the lake. While it seems that the lake-dwellers probably used this fruit for food, the piles of seeds are so numerous and large that the berries must have been used for something else as well perhaps to produce an alcoholic drink by leaving them to ferment.

Early Grain types and flint sickle

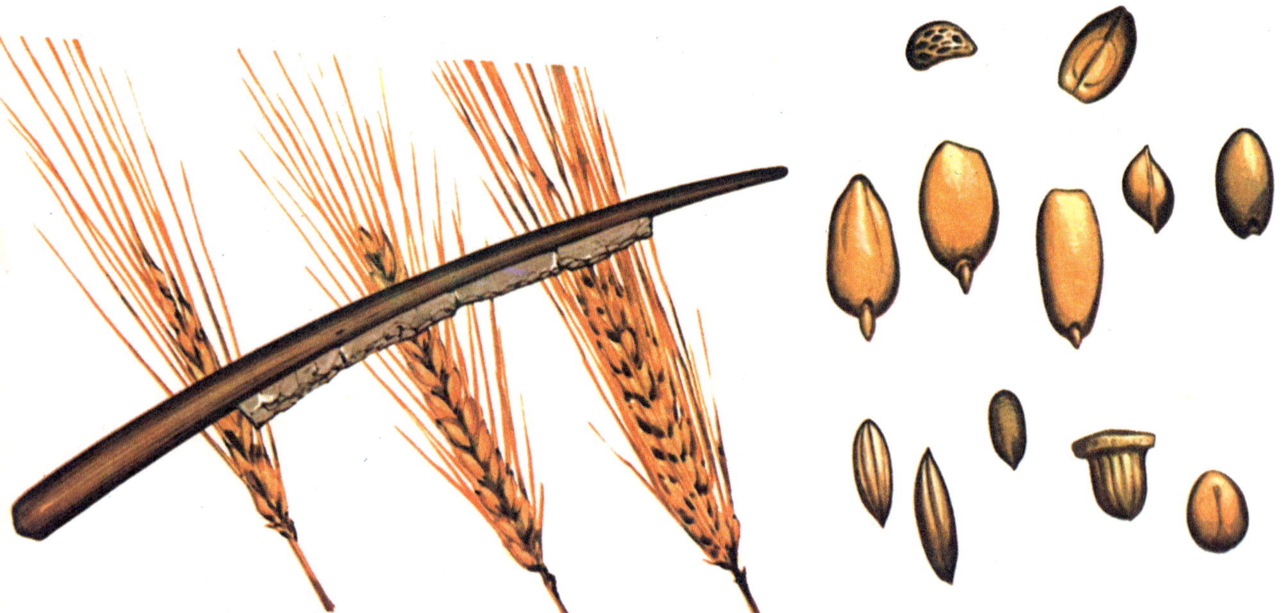

When corn was first grown

What is a grain of corn? It is something very small, only a few millimetres long and weighing only a few milligrammes. But if it is put in the ground in the right conditions, the seed swells, puts out a little root, a small leaf, and gives birth to a new plant.

Within the space of a few months the grain multiplies: it becomes thirty or forty new grains, grouped in an ear, themselves ready to produce new plants and multiply.

This process must have so impressed primitive man that it encouraged him to become a farmer, so that he could have enough corn to eat every year. Corn-growing is very ancient: nobody even knows in which part of the world it began or from which wild species the modern cultivated plant is derived.

According to the most likely suggestion, corn-growing began by chance. In the earliest times the cave-dwellers only gathered the grains of barley, wheat and rye which grew wild in woodland clearings. As this food could be kept for long periods, they filled their hide sacks with it to take with them on their frequent wanderings through the forests.

Before leaving, however, they never forgot to scatter a few grains on the ground, to please the gods.

After the winter, when they retraced their steps, they were amazed to find that the grains they had left on the ground had taken root and had given rise to new plants with swollen ears of corn. Perhaps this was how man learned to sow grain to grow new plants. And so some of the hunters became farmers, cultivating corn for themselves and their families.

The corn was eaten just as it was, in grains, or roasted over the fire. Bread-making was still unknown but it appears to have developed quite soon as cakes of barley have been discovered in Stone Age dwellings. Baking was practised by the ancient Egyptians. The Romans established public bakehouses from which free bread was distributed.

Early and late maize; squash

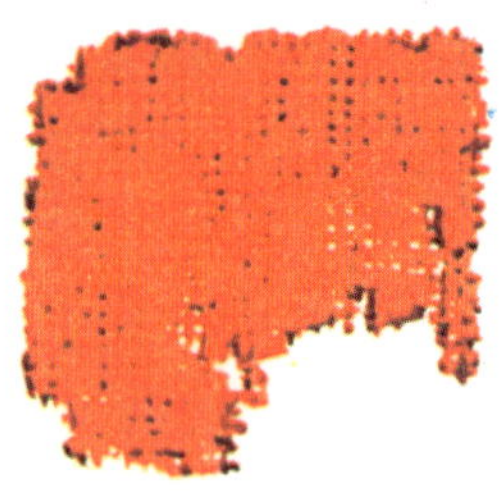

Textile, Halicar

When cloth began

In the Egyptian tombs paintings have been discovered which illustrate the cultivation of flax and the preparation of flax fibres for weaving into linen cloth. Linen must have been widely used in those days: the shrouds in which the mummies in the Pharaohs' tombs are wrapped are made of this material. The flax plant was therefore known in early times.

The use of hemp for making cloth and ropes also has very ancient origins. This plant was grown in China for its textile fibres as long ago as 2800 B.C. The fibres are coarser than those of flax and so are often stronger, which is why they are also used for making ropes and matting, as well as fabrics.

Hemp is a bushy-looking plant with stems of about 2 metres long and leaves with sharp-toothed edges. The flowers are either male or female and occur on separate plants.

When the olive became known

When Noah, the sole survivor of the Great Flood, saw the dove flying back to the ark with an olive branch in its beak, he knew that God's anger was appeased. So the story in the Bible goes and ever since the olive has been regarded as a symbol of peace.

There are many ancient books which quote the olive as one of the plants best-known to man and most closely answering his needs. This shows that the olive tree has been grown for thousands of years.

In the Palace of Knossus at Crete, dating back to 3,000 years before Christ, enormous jars have been found which were used for collecting and storing oil. The Greeks were great olive-growers and introduced the tree to Italy, along the Mediterranean coast.

The olive lives for a very long time, sometimes for thousands of years, but it never grows very tall. Its trunk is often gnarled and twisted and its leaves are a silvery green in colour because of all the tiny grey scales which shine on their undersides. The fruit of the olive is called a drupe: it is like a small fleshy plum, rich in oily substances, with a stone in the middle. While green the fruit can be bottled in brine. Olive oil is extracted from the ripe fruit.

The warmth of the Sun is vitally important if the olive is to grow. That is why this plant is better suited to southern countries or to a warm temperate climate, and is only rarely found in the northern countries. In California and in Arizona there are vast olive plantations.

Apart from the common olive, there are about fifty other varieties of the olive family.

An olive grove with detail of the fruit and leaves

When men learnt to produce wine

The cultivation of the vine in the Mediterranean basin has very ancient origins, and the art of producing wine is just as old. It is mentioned several times in the Bible, which refers to the grape as one of the Earth's greatest gifts to man.

Particularly expert in viniculture were the peoples of southern Italy, so much so that the Greeks called this part of the Italian peninsular *Enotria*—the land of wine.

It seems probable that in Italy the vine existed in a wild form even before the appearance of man, and it is certain that the first inhabitants of the peninsular ate the grapes they found in the woods, although they did not know how to cultivate them.

There is evidence, almost certainly reliable, of viniculture in Sicily as long ago as 2000 B.C. From Sicily it spread to other regions, and increased rapidly with the expansion of the Roman Empire.

During the Middle Ages it was monks who were the specialists in the cultivation of vines. Then the grapes spread again in the eighteenth century, when the worst vine diseases were identified and combatted.

Today Europe – principally France, Italy and Spain – is the world's main wine-producing region, followed by Russia, Argentina and the USA. Because there are many types of grape, there are also many wines on the market.

European wines are generally most favoured for their taste and bouquet, because most American vines do not produce very high-quality grapes.

When the pomegranate became known

The pomegranate bush which can grow to a height of 6 metres, is a native of subtropical Asia.

For thousands of years the strange fruit of this bush has been regarded as one of the most important fruits of the Mediterranean region. It is mentioned in the Bible and also figures in mythology.

Its sweet juicy seeds, like rubies in colour, and its beautiful bright red flowers have been an inspiration to authors and poets. The Italian poet, Carducci, wrote of ' . . . The green pomegranate yonder with crimson blossoms bright.'

In addition to the many varieties of fruit produced and grown, there are some 'full bloom' varieties of the shrub which bear beautiful double flowers but no fruit and are therefore only grown for ornament.

The pomegranate belongs to the Punicaceae family.

When the Romans brought new plants with them

The Romans did not only take their language, laws, dress and way of life with them on their conquests. Reminders of their passing are not only to be found in imposing palaces, roads, monuments and aqueducts scattered throughout their Empire. They also left their mark on the countryside, where they introduced new plants, and on the landscape of the hills, where they spread new species of trees.

The veterans of the victorious wars of expansion were given part of the conquered land as a reward for service and there they settled, devoting themselves to tilling the fields.

Vegetables and trees which they had grown in their native Latium were thus transplanted and spread wherever the climate permitted.

One of the most typical plants spread by the Romans is the cypress *(Cupressus),* a conifer originating from south-west Asia which spread rapidly from Greece to Italy and thence to the whole of Mediterranean Europe. Another tree very dear to the Romans was the domestic pine, with its peculiar umbrella shape; introduced into Italy by the Etruscans and once very common.

On the other side of the Mediterranean, in the hot African regions, the Roman rulers spread the banana, a fruit which was never missing from important banquets. The plant was already much prized by the Greeks who had been growing it since the days of Alexander the Great. In fact, it was the great Macedonian conqueror himself who had discovered its existence in the steaming jungles of India and had had it transplanted back home.

When the camellia was introduced into Europe

In the nineteenth century, poets and romantics were inspired by the delicate colours of camellia petals. The camellia was a very fashionable flower, fairly widespread in regions with a mild climate. It originated from eastern Asia and had been introduced into Europe around 1700.

The camellia was named by the Swedish botantist Charles Linnaeus after Georg Kamel (Camellus), a Moravian Jesuit who lived 1661–1706 and wrote a history of the flora of Luzon.

Gardeners vied with each other in attempts to grow the most beautiful varieties and specimens in the grounds of the stately mansions.

Nowadays this flower is no longer in such demand, but it has adapted perfectly to our climate and is to be found in many old

gardens.

The camellia flowers in spring. The plants, which may sometimes grow to as much as 7 metres tall, become covered with splendid pink, white or red blooms set among the dark green of the glossy leaves. The flowers have a strange habit: they are nearly always to be found on the back of the twisted branches. They may grow singly or in small groups and are normally unscented.

The best known and hardiest species is the *Camellia japonica* which was introduced into England from Japan in 1739 and of which there are now many single- and double-flowering varieties.

It is seldom realized that tea is obtained from another species of the camellia which is grown mostly in China, Sri Lanka and in India.

Another useful product is a domestic oil found in China and Japan and obtained by pressing the seeds of the *Camellia oleifera.*

When tea-drinking became popular

The raw material for making a good cup of tea, the infusion of tiny dark tips in boiling water, comes from the tender leaves of an ever-green plant which still grows wild in Burma and Assam.

Left to grow freely, the tea plant may reach as much as a height of 9 metres but on the plantations it is kept to not more than one metre, to make leaf-plucking easier.

Picking is done two or three times a year and is restricted to the shoots and tender leaves. These contain a stimulant called caffeine and a large percentage of tannin.

Green tea, which is drunk in China and Japan, comes from leaves which have only been dried. The Indian tea which is the kind mainly drunk in this country, comes from leaves which have been fermented as well as dried.

The leaves have a different aroma depending on the area where the plant was grown. The best teas are produced in the hills. Tea-plants like the shade and are usually grown under rows of spreading trees.

Tea-drinking, which is common in the East, was introduced into Europe by the Dutch around 1600.

When tea was first sold publically in London in 1657, England was the greatest coffee-drinking country in the world. Tea rapidly gained in popularity, although at first it was only obtainable by wealthy people, until by the mid-twentieth century twice as much tea as coffee was consumed in this country.

Today the biggest tea producers are India, Sri Lanka, China, Japan and Russia.

When tulips were precious flowers

There is a big family of plants called the Liliaceae. It includes not only the lily but 4,000 other species as varied as the buttercup, garlic, onion, hyacinth, aloe, yucca, asparagus, lily-of-the-valley, tulip and aspidistra.

Tulips are among the best known and most common Liliaceae today but a few centuries ago they were rare and were very precious, expensive flowers.

Grown for thousands of years in Turkey, where more than 1,300 varieties were known, they did not arrive in Europe until the second half of the sixteenth century. They achieved their greatest popularity in the eighteenth century, when there was not a garden, however humble or however grand, which did not include them.

Vast sums were spent on acquiring rare varieties of the bulbs. Today tulip-growing is an industry, particularly in Holland, which is the largest producer.

When cocoa was brought back to Spain

It was Columbus who, on his fourth voyage in 1502, took cocoa beans back to Spain. The Spaniards made them into a drink, adding sugar, but it was nearly 100 years before the use of cocoa spread to other parts of Europe.

Cocoa is obtained from the roasted seeds of a large fruit which ripens directly on the trunk or branches of a tropical plant. The Indians made it into drinks, mixing it with vanilla and spices, or made biscuits by kneading it with maize. They even used it as money in trade.

The cacao tree has large oval leaves. It can grow to 12 metres high but is usually pruned to between 4 and 8 metres. Small pinkish, wax-like flowers are produced on the trunk and the oldest branches. From these the pod-like fruit develops. It is up to 25 centimetres long, containing a white or pinkish pulp surrounding the seeds, which are a little bigger than our hazel-nuts. To reach the floury kernel in each seed, the tough pod which protects it has to be broken.

Each fruit may contain about thirty seeds called cocoa beans. They are first separated from the pulp then cleaned before being roasted. The roasting heightens their aromatic flavour and makes it easier to reduce them to powder. Special machines then release the cocoa from the tough skin and grind it up, at the same time separating part of the natural fat or cocoa-butter which is used for making such things as soaps and cosmetics.

Nearly 2 million tons of cocoa are produced a year, mostly in Brazil and West Africa.

When Charles V refused a pineapple

One of the most exotic fruits to arrive in Europe after the discovery of America was the pineapple.

Partly because it was so difficult to keep and partly because people were suspicious of it, the pineapple had to wait to conquer Europe until the arrival of rapid transport, the canning industries and mass advertising.

Even the Emperor Charles V of Spain refused to taste the first pineapple offered to him in case it was poisonous. Today, however, it is widely grown in all tropical countries where there is plenty of sunshine and warmth.

The first Europeans to mention the pineapple were Christopher Columbus and Sir Walter Raleigh who found it growing in the West Indies. In America it was already grown by the Indians, who had introduced it into many regions.

About 20 centimetres long, the pineapple looks something like a pine-cone. It grows on spikes rising from the centre of the plant. Botanically, it is a multiple fruit, like the blackberry and the strawberry. The plant, with its elongated, prickly leaves, only fruits after its third year.

When America gave us new food

Before the discovery of America, nobody in Europe had heard of maize. In fact, sweetcorn, which is unripe ears of maize, was unknown over here until it was imported from the New World, where it was intensely cultivated by the Indians.

They were already producing several types of Indian corn but later varieties have increased the number of seeds and improved the quality of the cobs.

Even more important than Indian corn was the arrival in Europe of a strange edible tuber called the potato. A native of Chile and Peru, the plant was found by the Spaniards on their first explorations of the South American continent. They took it home with them, together with other strange vegetables. By the end of the seventeenth century it was a major crop in Ireland and a hundred years later was widely grown in Europe, especially in Germany and in the west of England.

Other important vegetables introduced into Europe as a result of the discovery of America are red and green peppers, certain species of cucumber and beans and tomatoes.

When spices were worth more than gold

The precious spices from which seafaring republics had made their fortunes were known and used in Europe in the earliest times but their origin remained a mystery. Normally it was the Arab merchants who supplied them to European traders, but those cunning adventurers had never disclosed the source of their merchandize.

It was only with the great voyages of discovery that the origin of nutmegs, cinnamon and cloves was revealed.

Cloves were found by the Dutch in the Molucca Islands. For a long time attempts were made to prevent specimens of the clove-tree being 'stolen' for transplantation in other colonial territories, but in the · eighteenth century clove-growing spread rapidly to all the other tropical regions. Today there

are extensive clove-plantations in Madagascar, where the spice was introduced by the French.

When the plants are in flower, their strong scent can be smelt up to 300 kilometres away from the coast.

Cinnamon-growing is also widespread in many hot countries today.

Cinnamon comes from the bark of a tree which grows wild in India and Sri Lanka. It is the oil of cinnamon which produces its flavour: this is prepared from pieces of bark which are soaked in sea water and then distilled. A few centuries ago it was so precious that powerful nations actually went to war over the control of its production. The island of Sri Lanka passed from Portuguese to Dutch and then to British rule because, for trading reasons, each of these countries wanted to gain possession of its cinnamon groves.

The best known and most used spice is still pepper. In the Middle Ages the black berries of this sharp-tasting seasoning were so valuable that several people suggested using them as money for trade. A native of the moist, low-country forests of Sri Lanka and Southern India, the pepper plant is a creeping vine which is normally trained up other trees.

Its large leaves, arranged alternately, have almost no stem. Its flowers are joined in hanging spikes and produce round fruits, first green and then red. If picked at the red stage and left to dry, they become black and wrinkled and make black pepper. But if left to ripen fully, the pepper fruits turn brown and produce a single round seed inside them. When husked this seed makes white pepper, which tastes less sharp.

When coffee came to London

A third of the coffee drunk in the world today comes from plantations in Brazil but the plant is really of African origin.

It used to grow wild in the regions around the Red Sea and was first popularized in the Middle East by caravans of Arab merchants, although the drinks they prepared from it were somewhat different from the coffee we know today.

Coffee was introduced into Europe during the sixteenth and seventeenth centuries. It gained its first real popularity in the coffeehouses of London, the first of which was established in about 1652.

Coffeehouses flourished in the major cities of Europe and North America later in the 1600s.

By the end of the eighteenth century, the cultivation of coffee had spread to all the tropical regions, particularly America.

The coffee plant is a shrub which does not like the direct rays of the sun when it is growing. For this reason, neat rows of other shade trees, such as the acacia, are normally also grown on the plantations.

When wild the coffee-tree may grow up to 8 metres tall but the cultivated kind is pruned to a height of 2 to 3 metres. It has dark green, glossy leaves, oval in shape, and its white, scented flowers bloom in clusters in their axils. The flowers are replaced by green cherries which ripen to scarlet and contain two beans inside which are the seeds.

When roasted and ground, these seeds produce coffee powder. The drink we make from it contains caffeine, a drug which stimulates the heart and nervous system.

When tobacco was a medicinal plant

'Sovereigne herbe' was what our ancestors called tobacco in the sixteenth century. It had been found in tropical America, where the natives had been growing and smoking tobacco for thousands of years.

In Europe it was valued first as a medicinal plant and only taken as snuff.

Tobacco was also called 'Nicotiana' in honour of the French ambassador, Jean Nicot, who helped make it known by presenting a few seeds of the plant to Queen Catherine of Medici. The habit of smoking tobacco spread fairly slowly, however.

Cigars and cigarettes are prepared from the leaves of the plant, specially dried and cured to improve its properties. Numerous varieties of tobacco are grown today.

Hevea brasiliensis

Trunk being tapped for latex

Latex channels

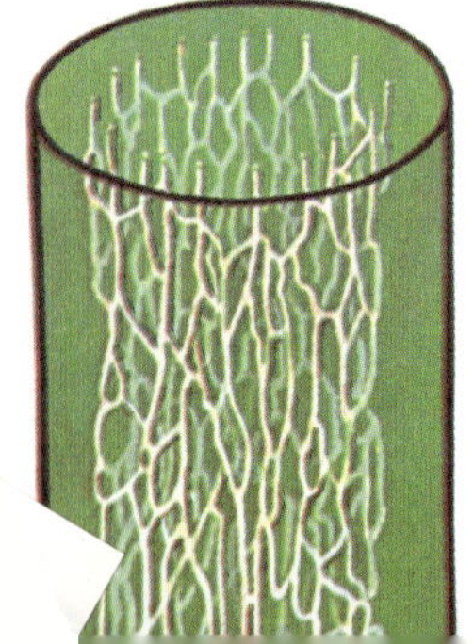

The tiny seeds are usually sown first in special nursery-beds. When the seedlings are about 10 centimetres high they are planted out in fields by hand or by special machines.

Left to itself, tobacco grows up to 2 metres high and produces pink or bright-red tube-shaped flowers. But the grower ensures that this does not happen by pruning the plants so that only the leaves develop, as this is the part used by the tobacco industry.

When the rubber tree became indispensable

Most of the rubber used in the world today is produced synthetically by the chemical industry. Until the last century, however, the only source of supply was a plant which provided it in the form of a sticky, milky juice called latex.

There are a wide variety of plants producing rubber but the best known tree and the one most grown for its rubber crop is the *Hevea*. It is a native of Brazil but there are also extensive plantations of it in Asia, where it was imported in the nineteenth century.

It is a very tall tree with a straight trunk and beautiful palm-like foliage. The crude rubber is obtained by cutting the bark and collecting the latex, which congeals in brownish lumps. It was used by the natives before the discovery of America.

One odd point is that the first rubber came to Europe in the form of bottles. The natives made them by covering a clay mould with several layers of latex which they left to harden over a smokey fire and then broke away the clay.

In 1736 rubber was taken to France by the physicist de la

Condamine, but it did not become really important until the nineteenth century when the vulcanization process was discovered and perfected by an American, Charles Goodyear, in 1839. In this process the rubber is treated with sulphur or sulphur compounds and becomes much tougher and more elastic, with the result that it can be used in a wide variety of industries.

It is called rubber because one of its earliest uses in Europe was erasing pencil marks.

When citrus fruits became known

Citrus fruits are oranges, lemons, lime, citron and grapefruit.

They are ever-green plants which are nearly all natives of the tropical regions of the Far East.

Oranges have been cultivated from early times and spread to India, the east coast of Africa and the eastern Mediterranean region. By the middle of the first century A.D. orange trees were being grown in Italy.

According to some sources, the citron was the first citrus fruit to be known on the shores of the Mediterranean. It resembles a lemon and was imported into Palestine from Persia by the Hebrews.

The Arabs introduced the lemon and the sour orange into Europe in the tenth century, while the sweet orange was made known to the Portuguese in the sixteenth century by Vasco da Gama who brought back a root of the tree from China.

Historical records of the citrus fruits and how they spread to other countries are rather uncertain. The only definite date refers to the tangerine: it was imported into England and Malta in 1805. Soon

160

afterwards it went to Palermo and in 1816 to Naples, whence it became widespread.

Citrus trees need a warm, temperate climate, not unlike that of their native land. They cannot therefore be grown outside a certain latitude. The Mediterranean climate has proved particularly suitable for their cultivation.

The plants were first grown in the gardens of villas as curiosities and for ornament. Their agricultural value and use as important fruits only began in the eighteenth century in Sicily and towards the middle of the nineteenth century in the Naples region of Italy.

When quinine was a mysterious medicine

The most valuable and sought-after part of the cinchona tree is its bark. When crushed into powder it makes quinine, which has proved to be a highly effective treatment for malaria.

Quinine is the most important alkaloid of cinchona bark. It is a white powder, odourless, crystallizable, bitter and poisonous. It can drive away fever, but if taken in heavy doses can cause serious upsets.

Cinchona trees are natives of the Andes, from Bolivia to Peru. There they were discovered or, rather, rediscovered in the sixteenth century by the Spaniards accompanying Pizarro who were shown how to use the medicinal properties by the natives.

Up until the end of the seventeenth century the origin of cinchona bark was kept a close secret in Europe, so much so that Louis XIV was prepared to pay 2,000 gold louis and a big income to the Englishman Talbot if he would tell him how he obtained such a miraculous medicine.

Later on, extensive cinchona plantations were established in Java by the Dutch. As a result of their skilful cultivation, Java became the world source of cinchona bark and, therefore, of quinine.

When the Japanese occupied Java during the Second World War the Allies' supplies of quinine were cut off. This led to the development of a number of new antimalarial drugs.

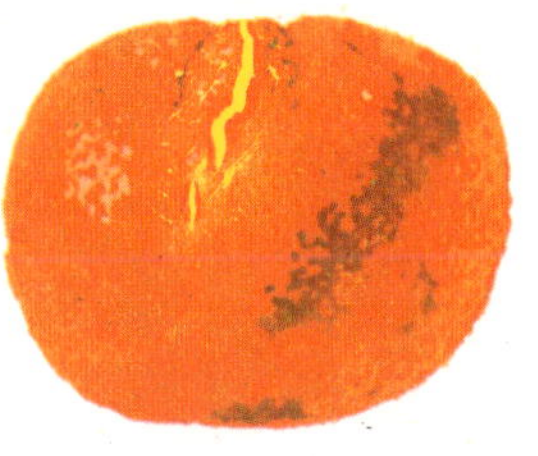

When sugar-beet became important

Sugar-beet suddenly became an important crop in the days of Napolean Bonaparte. In 1811 he developed its use to make up for the lack of sugar in his country during the continental blockade of France by the other European nations.

Before that, all the sugar consumed in the world came from the stems of a plant known as sugar-cane which only grows in hot countries. But by 1750 Germany had already begun to experiment in extracting sugar from the thick roots of the sugar-beet. Nowadays sugar-beet almost completely replaces sugar-cane in Europe and a quarter of the world's supply of sugar is derived from the root of the beet.

The sugar-beet is a biennial plant, which means that its roots thicken in the first year, storing all the nutritional substances which make the plant flower and bear fruit in the second year.

But before this happens, the sugar-beet is pulled out of the ground and sent to the sugar refineries. The leaves of the plant are used as cattle-fodder.

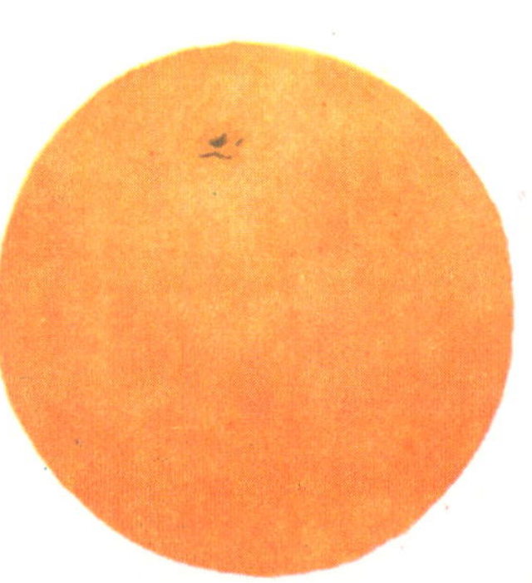

Royal Fern,
Osmunda regalis

Marsilea

Moonwort,
Ophioglossum

When a plant emigrated with a moth

Today the ailanthus tree is common throughout the Mediterranean regions, where it is regarded as a weed. It thrives wild everywhere, in the hedgerows and along railway banks, in neglected backyards and even through the ruins of tumble-down houses.

Yet until little more than a hundred years ago nobody in Europe knew of this plant. The story of its arrival in these regions is a strange one.

Towards the middle of the last century a serious crisis occurred in silkworm breeding in Europe. A mysterious illness attacked the caterpillars and killed them before they could finish their cocoons.

The epidemic threatened to make silk disappear from the markets, and silk in those days was a very important raw material on which the activities of many industries depended.

Some scholars then announced that in some areas of China the silkworm was successfully replaced by the *cynthia bombyx*, a large moth caterpillar which produced a voluminous cocoon of clear silk. This caterpillar could save the day.

A team of specialists left immediately and in 1856 the first eggs of the famous moth arrived in Europe, together with many young specimens of the ailanthus, the plant on which the caterpillars were to feed.

Experiments were made in several regions and the plants thrived everywhere, finding the European climate completely to their liking. Hopes were dashed, however, by the cynthia caterpillar which turned out to be somewhat unreliable and incapable of producing silk of a uniform quality.

In the mean time the epidemic which had attacked the silkworm had been overcome and so nobody tried to breed cynthia moths again.

But the ailanthus was by then healthily settled in southern

Europe and has since become so acclimatized and common as to be a nuisance.

The famous cynthia caterpillar continues to feed on its leaves, changing into a beautiful moth with a wing span of 15 centimetres which flutters round the houses at nightfall.

The wood of the ailanthus tree is also valuable to cabinet makers.

When there were giant ferns on the Earth

There are at least 6,000 species of fern which grow in various parts of the world, particularly in equatorial regions. But millions of years ago these plants grew in even greater profusion and reached gigantic proportions.

Particularly during the Carboniferous Period the forests were dominated by great tree-ferns, whose huge trunks gradually became changed into fossil coal. Traces of many species of fossil ferns are still to be found in lumps of coal, as they are in many clayey stones.

Today the size of ferns is somewhat more modest. Specimens up to 2 metres tall are to be found in tropical forests but in this country, in damp woods and valleys where they usually grow, these plants are at most 60 centimetres tall.

One of our prettiest ferns is the maidenhair, a little plant with a delicate frond pattern which grows in cool, shady places, often along rocky walls where there is a trickle of water. But the best-known ferns in our woods are the bracken, which covers the ground with its triangular-shaped, feathery fronds, and the male fern. This is a common British fern with long, narrow fronds and petioles, or leaf-stalks, covered with tufts of brown down.

Some other ferns which are particularly unusual are the arboreous ferns of the tropics which can grow up to 18 metres high; the so-called Antler fern owes its name to the fact that it produces two roughly circular fronds on a tree trunk, and from these sprout fertile fronds similar in shape to a deer's antlers. The *Marsilea*, on the other hand, is found mostly in shallow water and produces four small leaves on the top of a long stalk. It looks rather like a four-leaf clover.

When the plants joined forces with medicine

Some of the most interesting remedies used by medicine are the medicinal herbs which have provided man with important anti-dotes to diseases since time immemorial.

Around A.D. 1300 herbalists were influenced by a strange idea known as the Doctrine of Signatures. This theory maintained that the shape of the leaves, fruits and flowers of a plant were a sign of the disease which the plant could cure.

For example, heart-shaped leaves and flowers were recommended for treating heart diseases. Poppy heads were said to cure headaches and the lungwort lung diseases. The liverwort was used as a liver tonic because the shape of its leaves and the plant itself looked like a liver. The walnut kernel, similar in shape to the human brain, was recommended for curing mental diseases. Euphrasia with its black, pupil-like spot was thought to be good for the eyes, and similarly, yellow tumeric for curing jaundice.

Nobody nowadays believes in the Doctrine of Signatures, but scientists still search for medicinal plants and pay special attention to herbs used by primitive peoples and witch doctors.

When the giant sequoia were born

Sequoia, a genus of conifers, are well known for their gigantic size and their very long life span. In the United States and in Canada where they grow, the tallest and oldest examples are carefully protected.

There are two types of sequoia—the giant and the evergreen (but the giant type also keeps its green leaves in the winter).

The biggest in existence is the General Sherman which is nearly 4,000 years old and is 83 metres tall. Its diameter at the base is about 9 metres.

Evergreen sequoia do not live so long, but they are the tallest. The Founder's Tree, which is in California, is a good 110 metres tall. But its trunk is less massive: at the base it is four and a half metres thick. In Britain the sequoia rarely exceeds 30 metres in height.

The main difference in the two types of sequoia is in the shape and formation of the leaves. In the evergreen type they are needle-like, about one centimetre long; in the giant type the leaves are

A *Sequoia sempervirens* drawn to the same scale as Nelson's Column and the Statue of Liberty

much smaller, shaped like pointed bracts and arranged on the twigs like so many flat tiles.

Both types produce pines, but those from the evergreen are smaller and with a simpler shape. The trunks have a reddish bark, deeply lined, and a reddish wood which is light and tough and makes this a valuable timber tree.

When cotton began to be used as a textile fibre

The Greek historian, Herodotus, writing in the fifth century before Christ, claims that cotton was being used in India in 3000 B.C., and it is a fact that this material was first used in the East. It was grown and spun by the Egyptians in A.D. 600–700.

Some of the explorations of the fifteenth and sixteenth centuries were undertaken to gain additional supplies of cotton. When Vasco da Gama sailed round Africa in 1498, he found that Arab traders had long before taught the natives to cultivate and spin cotton.

When the European colonists discovered that the plant could thrive particularly well in the

The cone and leaf of the *Sequoia semper- virens*

climate of some areas of North and South America, cotton became increasingly important. The process of picking the locks of cotton from the bolls of the plants to weaving them into cloth is a long and complicated one. Today cotton is the most used of the plant textile fibres and the largest cotton crop is produced in America.

WHEN THE ANIMALS IN OUR LIVES BEGAN

In the far-off days of prehistory man's attitude towards the animals was entirely self-interested. He regarded them either as dangerous beasts, to be guarded against, or as precious sources of food, to be procured by hunting and fishing.

In either case, although he had no scientific interest in them, man was compelled to perfect his knowledge of the animals which lived on the plains and in the forests. For he could not avoid the wild beasts nor defend himself from their attacks and he could not catch his quarry without knowing their habits, their weaknesses, what they ate or where they slept.

Then, when man had caught his animal, it had to be cut up for food and skinned for its hide. And so he was taking his first lessons in anatomy.

The tribe's priests and sorcerers were in a way the first scientists, as it was their job to sacrifice the animals to please the gods. So they, better than anyone else, knew the anatomy of the victims they were cutting up on their altars.

A wonderful record of the interest that primitive man took in the animals, is provided by the beautiful rock-paintings discovered in several caves. The artists demonstrate an expert knowledge of the animals they were depicting.

Some animals have been man's faithful companions since the earliest times. Others have been domesticated and bred to produce meat, milk, eggs or skins. Still others have always been hunted as game. It is therefore natural to find frequent mention of animals in history, even in documents dealing with the most ancient civilizations.

Some peoples, however, have attached such importance to these creatures that they were thought to be incarnations of gods or devils, who were propitiated with ceremonies and sacrifices.

The gods of ancient Egypt are famous. A sacred cat was worshipped at Memphis and an ox at Thebes. Other cities worshipped wolves, jackals, lionesses, crocodiles, ibises and various fish from

the Nile. Many of these animals are portrayed in almost human form on the walls of the tombs, on the coffins and on the furniture in the funeral chambers.

Less well-known but equally important are the portraits of sacred animals, such as the plumed serpent, which appear in the sculptures of the ancient Mayan people.

When zoology began

We have to wait until the great Greek philosopher, Aristotle (384–322 B.C.), for the first serious attempt to bring together all the knowledge available on the animal kingdom.

Aristotle's merit is not just that he wrote five hefty treatises on all that was known about the animals in those days. He also made many original comments, discredited legends and described some 500 animals in amazingly accurate detail, even by today's more informed standards.

Yet, over the centuries, scholars became incapable of continuing and deepening Aristotle's work. They even distorted his writings to such an extent that new legends and ridiculous beliefs grew up and were handed on from people to people.

With the Romans the natural sciences made no progress at all. The only scholar to gather information on the animals was Pliny the Elder (A.D. 23–79), but his *Natural History*, written in thirty-seven books, is a mixture of useful comment and absurd legend. It contains many imaginary animals such as winged horses and unicorns and is certainly not of the same standard as Aristotle's earlier work.

The Middle Ages encouraged the birth of strange beliefs and superstitions still more. It was even thought that one particular goose was born as the fruit of some coastal plants.

It was not until the Renaissance that scientific interest in the animals was revived and descriptive works were written again.

When the first animals were domesticated

Primitive man could not begin to be civilized until he learned how to domesticate, or tame, the animals. Until then, he had to wander through the forests hunting game and tracking prey and he was forced to embark on long journeys to follow the animals which migrate.

As soon as he learned to keep a few animals, to use their milk, eggs, skins and meat, early man was able to build himself a permanent dwelling, to work with his hands and to farm the land around his hut.

The first animals bred by man might well have been birds. It was easy to find broods of baby birds in the trees or on the ground. They were caught and taken back to the hut, where they were fed and grew fat, laying a plentiful supply of eggs before they were killed and eaten.

Taming and breeding birds must have been much easier than catching and keeping a large mammal. The number of domestic species of birds known since antiquity shows that man began early in his history to breed birds.

A theory shared by Darwin was that all the domesticated breeds of poultry were derived from *Gallus bankiva*, a bird which inhabits northern India, Burma and parts of Malaysia. Darwin admitted, however, the lack of good evidence for this theory.

Pigeons, hens, ducks, geese and guinea-fowl all appeared on the table at banquets in antiquity.

Already in Roman times many types of domestic hen were known, and the guinea-fowl was bred by the Greeks who called it the African hen.

The peacock, too, was very highly thought of in Greece, where it had been introduced by Alexander the Great who discovered it in India.

It is also interesting to note that in the last few centuries there have been very few new domesticated animals.

The last large bird that was introduced to our tables, and especially at Christmas time, was the turkey.

In modern times man has shown a greater interest in machines than in animals.

When the dog appeared by man's side

Prehistoric rock carvings and cave paintings show scenes of hunting and daily life in the primitive villages. Often man is drawn with the dog by his side. It is the clearest proof that the dog was the mammal which first became accustomed to living near human dwellings, sharing the fate of the primitive peoples, accompanying them on hunting expeditions, helping them and defending them from the perils of the wild animals.

Several fossil dog skulls have been found near Stone Age camps and among the remains of lake-dwellings. The oldest remains of dogs in Europe have been found at Star Carr in Yorkshire. The breeds are different from the modern dogs but they are definite evidence of their long-standing friendship with man.

The freezes of Egyptian temples are also carved with figures of dogs as too are many early Egyptian monuments.

Cattle and sheep soon appeared near primitive villages, too, providing them with a valuable supply of food. They may have been brought into Europe by people who came from further east. When man succeeded in taming cows and sheep he took the first step towards stock-breeding.

A close companion of the sheep in prehistoric man's pens was the swine, the cousin of the wild pig. Near Stone Age camps in central and northern Europe, fossil remains of pigs have been found, together with those of goats and oxen. This is the earliest evidence of the domestication of pigs in Europe. In China they have been bred since 4,000 years before Christ.

When the cat 'walked by himself'

The cat is such a common domestic animal in our houses that it seems as if its friendship with man must date back to very ancient times, as does the dog's. But this is not so. Primitive man did not know the cat or, if he had occasionally met it in the woods, he thought of it as a dangerous meat-eater, of which he had to beware.

It hid in the trees and in the depths of the forests, living on prey like a tiger or any other fierce animal.

The first signs of its domestication are to be found before 2000 B.C. in the Egypt of the Pharaohs, where the cat was worshipped as a god. Nobody knows how it came

to Europe from Egypt, but we have a definite account of its presence in this continent towards the end of the Roman Empire. It is hardly mentioned in Greek, Roman or Jewish literature and at the beginning of the Middle Ages in Europe the cat was rare and costly. It had been known in China since A.D. 500 but it was not until the fourteenth century that it became a well-known household pet.

There are a number of varieties of domestic cat, an unusual one being the long-haired 'swimming cat' from Van in Turkey. It is chalk-white with auburn head-markings and a ringed tail, and is notable for its apparent liking for water.

When the beech-marten hunted house-mice

Until the fourth century after Christ the Romans did not know of the domestic cat. In its place, to rid themselves of mice, they kept tame beech-martens.

Relations between this animal and man are therefore very old but, apart from the exception of 'domestic' beech-martens, these relations have always been hostile.

This is not surprising as the beech-marten is a ferocious flesh-eater of the weasel family, which creates havoc in hen-houses and farmyards.

Unlike the marten, a close cousin which lives in woods and kills small wild animals, the beech-marten prefers to live in the open, using some abandoned ruin or old hut for refuge. It may often be found hidden in a stable, barn or wood-pile near the house.

From here it steals forth at night to creep into the hen-house where it goes completely berserk, slaughtering as many animals as it can. When it has finished it makes off, back to its lair, carrying a single fowl in its mouth. So it has no need to wreak such havoc among the poultry but the beech-marten is one of the fiercest and most blood-thirsty of carnivores and is hated and pursued by all farmers.

When the turkey came to Europe

For the people of the United States the turkey is a kind of national dish and is always served at traditional dinners, particularly on Thanksgiving Day. This feast celebrates the harvest and the other blessings of the past year.

The first Thanksgiving Day occurred in 1621. In a letter dated 11 December, Edward Winslow described how, when the harvest had been gathered, 'our Governor sent four men on fowling, that so we might after a more special manner rejoice together. . . . They four in one day killed as much fowl as . . . served the Company almost a week.' The 'fowl' were a large flock of wild turkey.

It was introduced into Europe at the beginning of the sixteenth century and since then roast turkey has become the traditional Christmas dinner in many European countries. The turkey has gradually increased in size as the breeds have been improved by selection and crosses. Today, a good farm turkey may measure as much as one metre twenty tall if it is a cock and slightly less if it is a hen. Turkey breeding can be a very profitable business and has become a large scale industry.

Wild turkeys still live in the forests of the United States. They are smaller than the domestic ones and live in huge groups, scratching the ground for berries, roots, worms and any other kind of food. They sometimes make long migrations to find new land for undisturbed grazing.

When the legend of the unicorn flourished

The ancient peoples of the Mediterranean believed in the existence of the unicorn, a mythical animal which was supposed to look like a horse with a long horn on its forehead. This story seemed to be confirmed by the first travellers to northern seas who brought back with them strange, spirally twisted 'horns' that they had found on the beaches of the mysterious northlands. Yet nobody had seen one of these mythical animals, dead or alive.

The legend of the unicorn stirred the imaginations of men until the late Middle Ages. Some people even tried to reconstruct the legendary animal by taking the skeleton of a horse and fixing one of those famous spiral horns to its skull.

But, with the beginning of scientific study based on the close observation of nature, these hoaxes were exposed.

In 1655, some sailors fished a narwhal out of the ocean and carried its skeleton back to Europe. It was clear that the long, twisted 'horns' discovered by the ancient travellers really belonged to this aquatic mammal and not to the unicorn at all. For the narwhal, a kind of whale, has a single large tusk, twisted in a left-handed spiral, which juts out horizontally from its mouth.

So the 'horns' found on the beaches were not from unicorns but were tusks of dead narwhals, washed ashore by the sea-currents.

When whales were terrifying monsters

Today everyone knows that the whale is not a fish but a mammal. Until the middle of the sixteenth century, however, even scientists thought it was a huge fish and knowledge of this animal was so slight that the strangest legends grew up.

One of these claimed that when the whale is resting motionless on the surface of the water it may be mistaken for an island, to the great danger of the sailors who land on it!

Whales are indeed exceedingly large but not as large as the ancients described. The sei whale, a small rorqual, or fin-back whale, grows to at most 21 metres long, a third of which is taken up by the head. Its mouth is immense, up to 6 metres long and 3 wide.

To obtain its food the whale swallows a mouthful of seawater and then, with its jaws closed and using its tongue like a piston, it drives all the water out, filtering it through the fringed plates which it has instead of teeth. Small fish and above all plankton remain trapped in the cetacean's mouth.

Turkeys

Chihuahua

Snakes

Grey squirrel

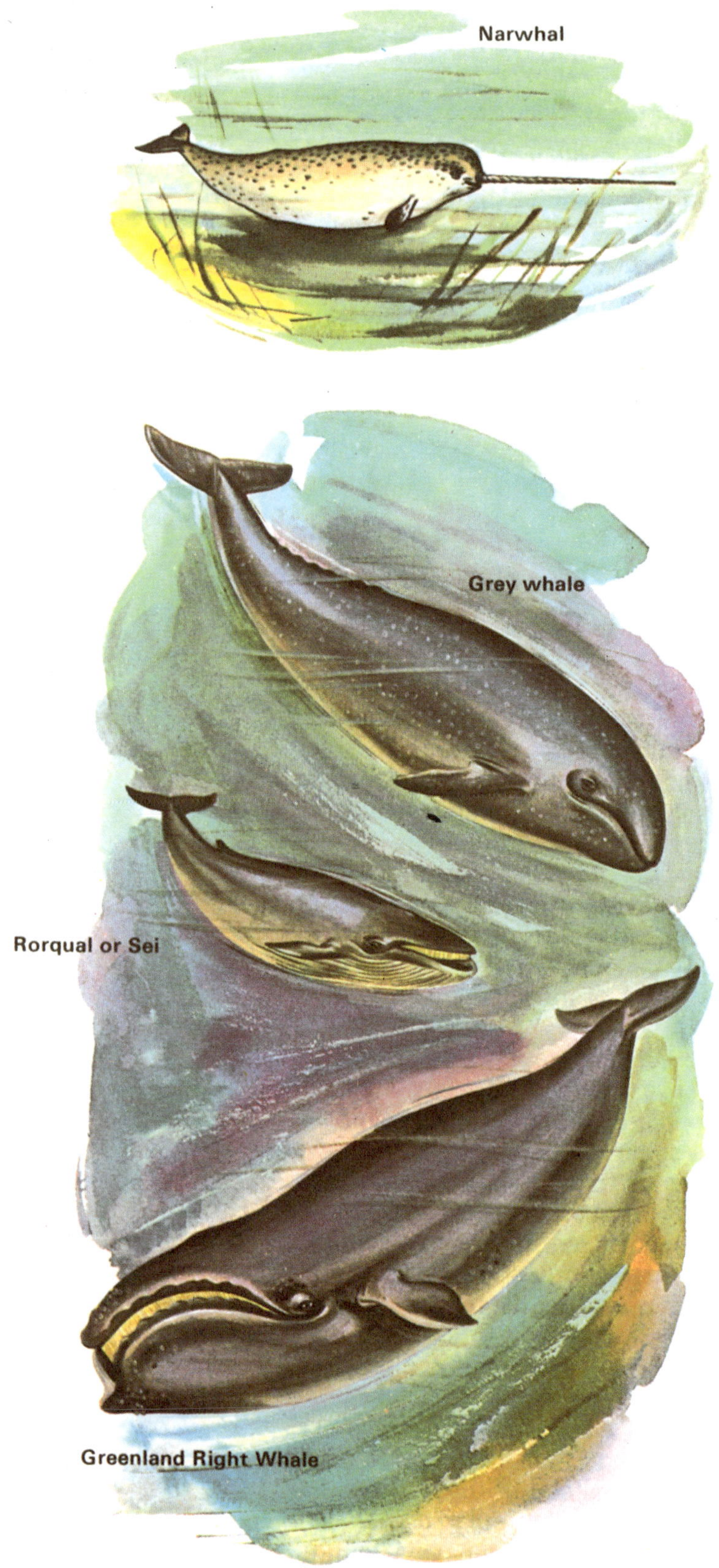

The gray whale of the northern Pacific can grow to a length of 15 metres. The beaked or bottle-nosed whale is the smallest of the whale family and grows to a maximum length of only 9 metres.

The female whale normally gives birth to only one baby whale, which is about 7 metres long.

Sei whaling by Europeans began when other whales, which used to frequent our local seas, became very rare because of the wholesale slaughter.

Since the beginning of history the Eskimos and Red Indians have managed to catch a few specimens of this aquatic mammal by a very difficult method. They row up to the animal in flimsy canoes, climb on to its head and drive two sticks firmly between its blowholes, making it die of suffocation.

The whaling ships were 200–300 ton vessels with square sails, a wide main beam and deep holds which could take up to 2,400 barrels of oil. They could be recognized from a long way off by their sails, which became stained by the brick ovens in which the whale fat was boiled to extract the oil. It was essential to have space to cut the whales up into sections, and so the cabin, normally in the prow, was moved astern.

The boats actually used for catching whales, were slim craft made of cedar and so light that two men could lift one. They could be rowed by five men at a speed of up to 10 knots.

In modern times whale fishing, chiefly of rorquals, has become so profitable commercially that the whale is in danger of being overfished, and international agreements limit the total kill.

When Cook's discoveries amazed the naturalists

In 1770 Captain Cook's sailors penetrated the interior of the Australian continent to look for fresh meat. They returned to the ship carrying some 'game' which astonished and intrigued the whole crew. What they had caught were big kangaroos, which no one had ever seen before.

Only found in certain parts of Australia, these strange creatures had never been heard of by zoologists and it was not until their chance discovery by the sailors that kangaroos became known to the world.

Today they have become the symbol of Australian animal life.

Their best-known feature is their pouch. The baby kangaroo spends much of its time in its mother's pouch, and even when it can run and jump it goes there for shelter and protection.

Kangaroos can grow to nearly 3 metres in length, including the tail. The head is small compared with the rest of the body and tapers forward. The shoulders and front legs, too, are feebly developed, but the hind legs and tail are long and powerful, so that these animals can leap forward and move swiftly.

They are plant-eaters and consume vast quantities of pasture, browsing on grass and various kinds of vegetation. It is for this reason as much as for sport that kangaroos are hunted, for the grass is needed for cattle and sheep.

By nature kangaroos are timid and inoffensive except when cornered and then they defend themselves with their sharp claws and powerful hind legs.

In the wake of Cook's voyages of discovery, incredible accounts of strange, sometimes incredible animals reached Europe.

For example, the skin of the first duck-billed platypus on record was taken to England in 1797. It gave rise to heated discussions, not to say violent quarrels, among scholars who did not know how to classify it.

The duck-billed platypus is indeed a strange mixture of bird and mammal. It has the bill and egg-laying habit of a duck but when the 'chick' hatches out the mother platypus gathers it up and suckles it, like an ordinary mammal.

And this is not all: the platypus has the tail of a beaver, which it can beat at swimming; it is cold-blooded, like a snake; it burrows underground holes like a mole and it waddles on land like a penguin.

Altogether, it seems to be a complete freak of nature.

Yet this creature really does exist and has kept scholars fully occupied, observing its habits and anatomy and looking for links with other creatures, alive or extinct.

The echidna, which is very rare, is a mainly nocturnal animal and lives in the sandy, rocky regions of south-east Australia and Tasmania. It is found in no other area.

Kangaroo

The echidna, or spiny anteater, as it is also called, is another inhabitant of the Australian continent which has attracted great interest and sparked off endless discussions.

It is a mammal but, like the duck-billed platypus, it lays eggs. The female echidna places her single egg in her pouch and suckles the baby there when it has been born.

It, too, is a strange mixture of characters belonging to animals of widely divergent species. It has sharp prickles like a hedgehog or porcupine, an elongated, sensitive snout like no other animal's, padded feet like an elephant's, strong claws and a worm-shaped, sticky tongue like an anteater's.

It has the same eating habits as an anteater, too, as it feeds solely on ants, catching them with its darting tongue. It uses its strong claws to dig up and turn out ants' nests, making the insects run.

This animal, like the porcupine, rolls itself into a ball when disturbed.

When the animals began to be classified

The first scholars to describe the animals living on Earth tried to group them according to certain common characters. They felt they must put the vast quantity of knowledge they had amassed into some sort of order.

Aristotle had already devised an important system of classification, in which he divided the animals into two main groups: those with blood and those without blood. We now know that all animals have blood, even if it is not always red, but in Aristotle's day knowledge of the animals was limited.

For another 2,000 years, scholars who came after him continued to classify animals more or less in the same way. It was not until 1700, with the development of anatomy, that the internal structure of animals began to be better understood.

At the end of the seventeenth century John Ray devised new classifications and these were further improved by Georges Cuvier in the early nineteenth century. These new classifications form the basis of those now used by modern science.

Echidna

Platypus

Since the middle of the eighteenth century, the two-name (binomial) system, devised by the Swedish botanist, Linnaeus, has been adopted for all classifications. In this system, the scientific name of each animal is always made up of two parts, the first indicating the genus, or subdivision of the family, and the second the species, which describes what the animal is like or where it is found.

When the great debate on the origin of the animals began

In the first half of the nineteenth century animal research made tremendous progress. But naturalists were divided into two opposing camps. On the one hand were the scholars convinced of the unchangeable nature of the various animal species. On the other were those who believed in the continual evolution of the animals and the tendency of the species to go on changing to adapt to their surroundings.

Scholars in the first group, called creationists, were supported by Linnaeus' theory that 'there are as many species as the different forms created by the Supreme Being at the beginning of time'.

The chief exponent of creationism was Georges Cuvier (1769–1832), the founder of comparative anatomy. He refused to accept the evidence showing that the animals which lived long ago were not the same as those living today.

When scientists believed in the theory of catastrophism

Cuvier was bitterly opposed to any theories contrary to his own, and his great prestige was one of the reasons why important discoveries were ignored. These discoveries would have shown how the animal kingdom evolved.

However he could not continue to ignore the discoveries of fossil remains of animals which had disappeared millions of years before.

In particular, these remains were always being found in certain layers of rock dating back to definite geological eras.

He explains this fact by the theory of catastrophism. According to this, at certain times in the history of the Earth, immense cataclysms occurred, changing the surface of the Earth and wiping out all sign of life. When calm was afterwards restored, a new act of creation repopulated the Earth with more advanced animal forms.

Following the same theory, another scientist, d'Orbigny, had even worked out as many as twenty-seven creations interspersed with twenty-six floods and universal catastrophes. This explanation could obviously not hold good for long, however.

Charles Linnaeus

Even in Cuvier's day, another great scientist, Jean Baptiste Lamarck, had put forward a scientific theory in a pamphlet he published.

It recognized that the animals living around us are the result of a continual evolution of primitive forms, due to the influence of climate, temperature and altitude.

At first his theory passed unnoticed but Lamarck's inspired guess soon became the basis of all modern zoological science.

When evolution became a certainty

Although Lamark's theory of evolution was to a certain extent correct, its weakness lay in its lack of definite scientific evidence.

Then, in 1859, a new event threw the zoology world into complete confusion. Just over twenty years earlier, Charles Darwin had returned from a long surveying voyage to South America and the Pacific. There he had collected some important material, and in 1859 he published his book *On the Origin of Species by Means of Natural Selection*. In it his observations on the slow change of the animals from the ancient primitive species to the modern ones were so well illustrated that the doctrines of the creationists crumbled for ever.

On one stage of his voyage aboard the *Beagle*, Darwin went to explore the Argentinian Pampas and came upon the fossil remains of enormous creatures which were bigger and more strangely shaped than anyone had believed possible. Later, on the Galapagos Islands, thousands of kilometres away from the coast of Ecuador, he discovered that geographical isolation had indirectly given rise to

Lamarck

new animal species.

He noticed in particular that the finches which live there form a family of their own, which is only to be found on the Islands and not on the South American mainland. They most probably all originated from a single pair which went to the Islands a long time ago and adapted to their environment by evolving into five genera and some twenty species. Each of them had developed different eating techniques and therefore differently shaped beaks.

These observations and those made from other animals from geographically isolated regions led Darwin to believe firmly in the evolution of species and to describe the mechanism of mutation.

Basically, Darwin said that in

every species the only individuals to survive and reproduce are the ones which are best fitted to defend themselves and adapt to their environment. This means that there is a continual process of natural selection which in time gives rise to new breeds.

Darwin

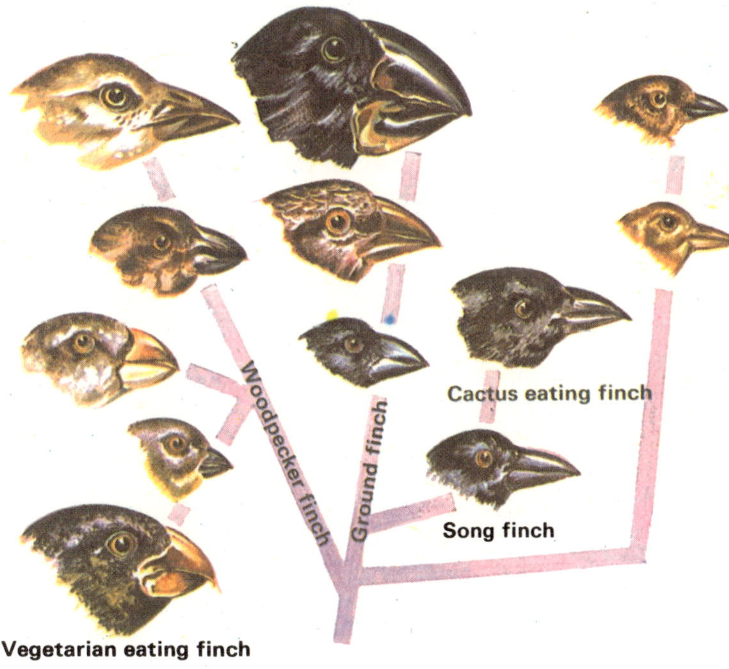

177

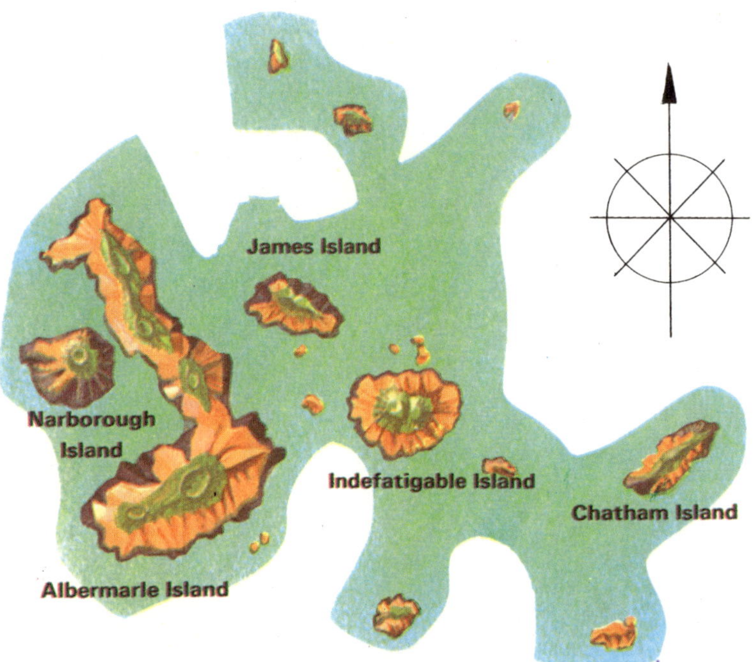

The Galapagos Islands: studying life on the thirteen largest islands shows that several genera of animals have formed separate species on different islands

When birds migrate across the world

The greatest travellers in the world are the birds, who move about from place to place in search of food.

Every autumn millions of them leave the places where they have bred or been born, and fly to other areas to spend the winter. The following spring they return to their breeding grounds.

Only during the nesting season do they stay in the place where they lay their eggs. For the rest of the year even so-called 'sedentary' birds make longish journeys, looking for new hunting grounds.

Some migrate regularly every year to very distant countries. The best known migrants are, of course, the swallows, which leave our shores at the end of the summer and fly to the warm regions of the south, to return to their own nests in the spring.

In the cloudy grey days of early autumn they gather restlessly along the telegraph wires. The groups form, break up and form again, stringing out across the wires like black notes on a line of music.

Then, one morning, their call does not come. The swallows have gone.

In fact, they are flying away towards Africa. An irresistible urge is carrying them towards their winter quarters where the climate is milder and there is food in plenty.

Like the swallows, other birds fly off for distant, more hospitable lands. Nearly all the insect-eating birds migrate as the cold kills the insects so there is nothing left for them to feed on.

The migrations start with the swifts, towards the end of July. Screaming and squealing around church towers and belfries, they sound the flight-call and soar up in huge flocks, heading towards the hills on their long journey to the south.

In October they are followed by the swallows. Flying high in the sky in neat formations, they disappear over the horizon along their regular route which for thousands of years has taken them to their winter quarters. With them go many other birds, some to the Mediterranean, some beyond.

Even some large birds which live on ponds or along streams migrate to the south when ice covers the water and stops them from finding their food.

Storks, ducks, cranes, geese, all migrate. They travel thousands and thousands of kilometres, flying high in the sky by night and day. They pass over mountains, cross plains and lakes, face the open sea and carry on until they reach their destination, where they have wintered for year after year.

They stay away for many months, then fly back in the opposite direction, to return to their nests as soon as the warm weather begins.

Of all the insect-eaters, only the woodpecker stays in our woods. He is not afraid of the winter; his strong beak can rummage in the bark of trees, where all the larvae are hidden, so he can find plenty of food, even in the coldest weather.

When migrations began to be studied

The migrations of birds have been known for thousands of years but their systematic study only dates back to the last century, when the Danish naturalist, Christian Mortensen, invented the ringing system.

The idea is simple. It involves catching a large number of birds alive and attaching a numbered metal ring to the leg of each, with the name of the bird observatory where it has been ringed. The birds are then let go to follow their normal migratory routes. Anyone catching one of these birds has to report it to the bird observatory, which can gain important information about the patterns of migration of each species from the place and time of capture.

The system has worked, although little more than one per cent of ringed birds are recovered. Bird observatories have spread and are now quite numerous.

By knowing which place the various birds have left and where they are caught, it is possible to plot the exact route they normally

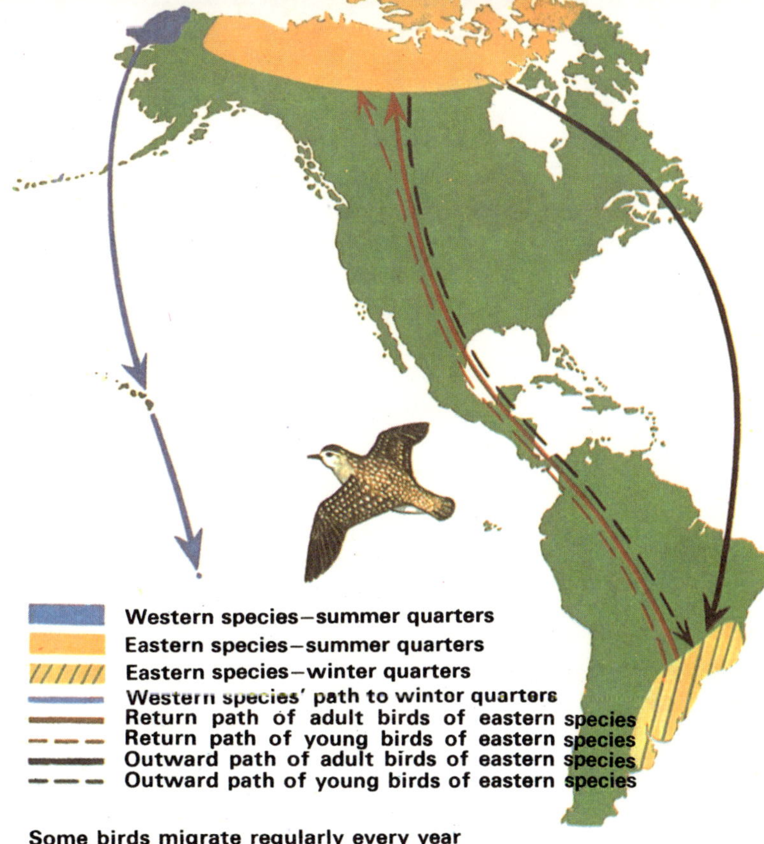

Some birds migrate regularly every year to very distant countries

The ringing system allows the routes which migratory birds normally follow to be plotted exactly

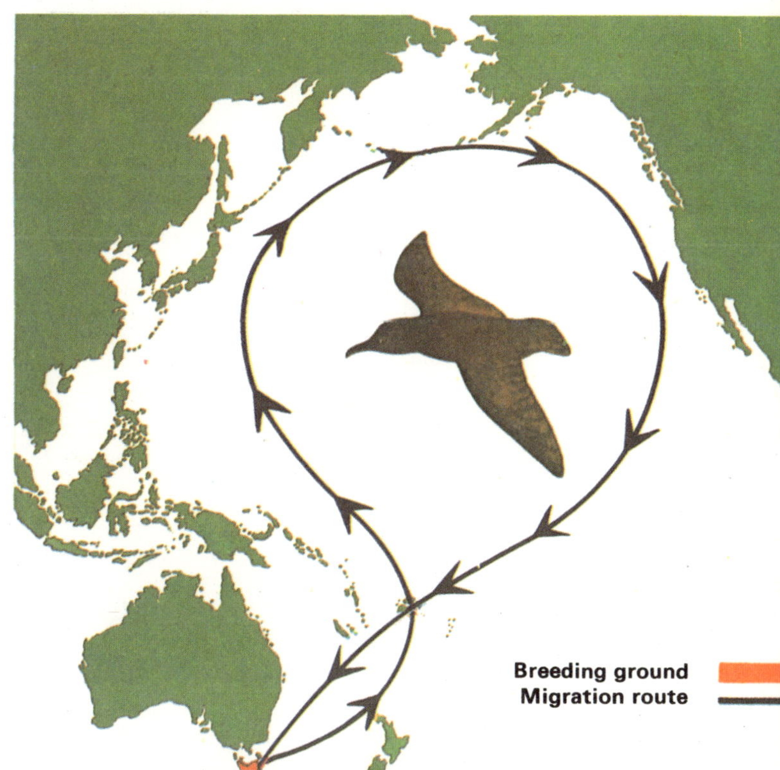

follow to migrate from north to south and back again.

It is also possible to work out the average flight speed, which is considerably slower than that of normal flight. A hawk, for example, can swoop down on its prey at 290 kilometres an hour but, when migrating, it does not fly at more than 77 kilometres an hour on average. Although swallows are high-speed birds, they do not cover more than 400 kilometres a day, taking five or six weeks on the outward journey and the same again on the return.

These journeys are naturally very tiring and dangerous. It is estimated that more than half the birds die before they reach their destination.

Today official protection is given to birds and bird sanctuaries exist in most European countries and in America.

When the bottom of the sea was first explored

In 1960, when Jacques Piccard went down 10,916 metres to the bottom of the sea in his bathyscaphe, the sight which met his eyes had never been seen by man before.

For some time past people had known about some of the deep-sea fishes, which had been caught in special nets, but they usually reached the surface dead and disfigured by the enormous difference in water pressure.

Nobody had ever seen them alive, swimming in their natural habitat in the mysterious depths of the sea, where not even the faintest glint of sunlight brightens the darkness.

The searchlights on Piccard's bathyscaphe lit up a fascinating scene. Strange and monstrous

Piccard's Trieste

creatures passed through the beam of light; fish with luminous spots along their sides, like a row of twinkling port-holes on an ocean liner; fish with huge bulging eyes; fish with transparent bodies like glass; monsters with enormous mouths and fearful pointed fangs; animals with the power to give electric shocks; small voracious fish which swallowed up prey five times bigger than themselves, blowing up their stomachs like balloons.

Unaware of the presence of the bathyscaphe, these terrifying creatures fought and devoured each other, driven by their insatiable appetite. As no plants can grow at such depths because of the absence of light, the fish are carnivorous. In colour they are very vivid, scarlet, violet, orange and purple being the predominant colours.

These animals are nearly always blind but they have a highly developed sense of touch and find their way to their prey with their long feelers.

Others have luminous spots on their bodies, not to see where they are going, as might be supposed, but to attract smaller fishes and save themselves the trouble of chasing them.

Not all of them are predators, however. Many of them also eat dead creatures catching in their wide jaws the debris which floats down to them from the upper water-layers of the sea.

Jacques Piccard's urge to explore the underwater depths was a family characteristic.

In 1953 his father Auguste had descended to more than 3,000 metres in the waters around the island of Ponza.

His bathyscaphe was a spherical steel cabin, 2 metres in diameter.

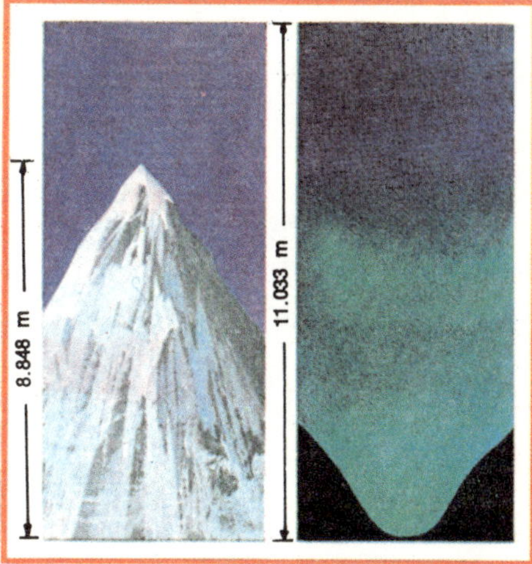

Diagram to show Mount Everest in relation to the depth dived by Trieste into the Marianas Trench

It was connected to a floating container filled with petrol which, being lighter than water, provides the necessary lifting power.

It also had its own means of propulsion and therefore did not have to be attached to a boat up on the surface, as had happened with the bathysphere.

The illustrations in this book are the work of the following artists:

D. Andrews, H. Barnet, M. Battersy, J. Bavosi, J. Berry, J. Beswick, G. Davies, Design Bureau, Design Practitioners Ltd., G. J. Galsworthy, R. Geary, G. and H. Green, R. Hargreaves, J. Hayes, N. W. Hearn, A. McBride, D. MacDougal, B. Melling, P. Morter, B. Mullick, J. Nicholls, K. Ody, A. Oxenham, G. Palmer, J. Parker, H. Perkins, B. Robertshaw, J. Smith, M. Shoebridge, B. Stallion, K. Thole, P. Thornley, R. Wardle, D. A. Warner, P. Warner, Whitecroft Designs Ltd., M. Whittlesea, W. Wright.